THE GOD OF FORGIVENESS AND HEALING IN THE THEOLOGY OF KARL RAHNER

J. Norman King
University of Windsor

UNIVERSITY
PRESS OF
AMERICA

231.0925
K583
82081323

Library of Congress Catalog Card Number: **81-40932**

To my father and mother,

George and Emma King

CONTENTS

INTRODUCTION

For Karl Rahner God is the inscrutable and holy mystery which we encounter in our deepest human experience. We touch upon God at the most profound level of our every human act. Yet we do so only implicitly, as we come into contact with the persons and things around us. This implicit experience of God is the transcendental dimension of our everyday experience. While usually remaining in the background, it breaks into the forefront of our awareness most forcefully in the crucial situations, events, and stages of human life. Among these Rahner mentions solitude, joy, anxiety, responsibility, love, death, guilt, truth, and beauty. Such occasions involve our entire self and confront us with the meaning of life as a whole. It is in our response to them that we stake our whole self and shape the fundamental direction of our life. These critical moments provide the basis for understanding what is meant by "God." From a Christian viewpoint the divine reality mirrored through them shines forth most fully in Jesus of Nazareth. In the light of his person, life, death, and resurrection, we may portray this mystery as the nearness of forgiving love.[1]

In the present study we shall explore one avenue of this experience of God: that offered by sin and guilt along with the hope of overcoming them by forgiveness and healing.[2] From this perspective God is viewed as that presence which a person ultimately betrays in violating his own or others' sacredness. God is also that presence towards which the guilty person ultimately reaches for a forgiveness and healing which

1

can only be received as gift.

Where Rahner deals specifically with the experience of God he alludes only briefly to sin and forgiveness and their particular contribution to our conceptualization of God. Nor does Rahner fully develop his treatment of God while discussing various aspects of guilt and its remission. In this book we shall attempt to bring together these two themes of Rahner's theology and thus to speak of the God of forgiveness and healing. Following Rahner's guidance we may in this way arrive at a richer understanding of the mystery to which the word "God" points, an understanding that is both grounded in experience and clarified by Christianity. Perhaps too we may contribute a little to the "mystagogy" or initiation into the experience of God which Rahner regards as vital for the age in which we live.[3]

We shall begin with a brief presentation of Rahner's view of the experience of God. Within this context we shall then elaborate the avenue of this experience found in sin and in the forgiveness of sin.

NOTES

[1]Karl Rahner, "The Experience of God Today," _Theological_ _Investigations_ 11 (London: Darton, Longman and Todd/New York: Seabury Press, 1974), 149-165; _Foundations_ _of_ _Christian_ _Faith_ (New York: Seabury Press, 1976), 24-43, 51-71, 448-459. Fifteen volumes of Rahner's _Theological_ _Investigations_ (hereafter abbreviated as _TI_), have been published in English translation from 1961 to 1979.

A brief statement of Rahner's basic vision is given in his summary expressions or "short formulas" of the essence of Christian belief. See "The Need for a 'Short Formula' of the Christian Faith," _TI_ 9, 117-126; "Reflections on the Problems Involved in Devising a Short Formula of the Faith," _TI_ 11, 230-244.

An excellent introduction to Rahner's _Foundations_ and to his overall thought is provided in Leo J. O'Donovan, ed., _A_ _World_ _of_ _Grace_ (New York: Seabury Press, 1980).

Unless otherwise indicated, all references are to the works of Karl Rahner.

[2]For a discussion of other avenues of the experience of God, see J. Norman King, "The Experience of God in the Theology of Karl Rahner," _Thought_ 53 (1978), 174-202. A much more extensive and concrete presentation is given in J. Norman King, _Experiencing_ _God_ _All_ _Ways_ _and_ _Every_ _Day_ (Minneapolis: Winston Press, 1982).

[3]On the topic of "mystagogy," see "Atheism and Implicit Christianity," _TI_ 9, 158-160; "Theological Considerations on Secularization and Atheism," _TI_ 11, 182-184; "Possible Courses for the Theology of the Future," _TI_ 13, 40-42; "Kirchliche und Ausserkirchliche Religiosität," _Schriften_ _zur_ _Theologie_ 12 (Zurich: Benziger, 1975), 593-596; _Foundations_, 57-61.

PART A: THE EXPERIENCE OF GOD

1.   THE EXPERIENCE OF INFINITE MYSTERY

In his more recent writings, Karl Rahner has increasingly stressed the importance of human experience, both personal and cultural, for theological reflection. Theology must draw upon, interpret, and
speak to modern man's understanding of himself. The
theologian is challenged to discover the connections
between Christian doctrines and this modern self-
understanding, and to formulate their correlation
clearly.[1]

Here, theology faces a severe challenge. The
person of today keenly feels the absence of God,
whether the absence evokes sorrow or apparent indifference. Nothing in a secular, pluralistic, and tech-
nological world seems to speak of God. The world
fashioned by modern hands projects only our own very
human image, and that image is often palpably and
painfully finite and mortal.[2] Yet for Rahner, the
experience of God is precisely the heart and center of
doctrinal Christianity and finds therein its clearest
and most complete articulation.[3] (Indeed, all religions "consist in the conceptual reflection upon and
social institutionalization of this experience of
God," which they achieve with varying adequacy.)[4]
Christian theology, therefore, has the urgent task of
pointing to this basic experience in a recognizable
way, within the context of contemporary life. Theology must forge a genuine conceptualization and interpretation where such understanding is lacking, inadequate, or erroneous.

In Rahner's vision, the experience of God is the experience of man's radical orientation to mystery. This human transcendence, as he terms it, belongs to the very structure of man; it is one of his permanent "existentials." In fact, it constitutes the very definition of the human being: openness to mystery. This orientation is implicit in and underlies every human act. It is, as it were, the frame on which is built and moulded the material of all other human experience of persons and things in the world. Rahner refers to the element which makes possible and structures all human experience as its a priori, transcendental dimension. He designates the actual concrete content of that experience as its a posteriori, historical dimension.[5] The transcendental orientation is most clearly discernable, once again, in the critical aspects of human existence, where the person is most alive to his own spiritual depths. To begin elucidating this position, let us look at the modern sense of the absence of God.

The failure to discover God may well result from a loss of self through thoughtless immersion in the cares, tasks, and affairs of everyday life. This absorption may spring in its turn from an evasion of ultimate questions, or from a despair over any final meaning to human life.[6] However, the failure to find God may be a step towards a more refined image of God. A naive theism tends to portray God as one individual existent being alongside others within the totality of the world, a God whom one might come across during his lifetime somewhat as one meets another person or thing. Many today may tacitly recognize that neither in whole nor in part is the world to be identified with God, that "no image of God can be carved from the wood of the world."[7] If God is a reality, God must be more in the background, so to speak, immeasurably more transcendent, awesome, and ineffable.

Moreover, the perception of oneself and everything within one's physical and social environment as finite precludes any facile discovery of God. An awareness of the utter contingency of all that one directly encounters and a refinement of the concept of God are complementary insights. Certainly, if the world is finite, it is not God. At the same time, Rahner maintains, modern man is acutely sensitive to this finiteness and suffers because of it. He is pained because he sees this finiteness in the light of an infinity, and this infinity is the real goal of all his strivings.[8] We see and measure everything that is finite in the light of an infinity, and we make every finite choice in view of this infinity. This infinity is the nameless and holy mystery called God. We must briefly expand this notion.

While we are sometimes weighed down by the limits of our existence, we may at other times be sustained by an unexpected peace or joy which seems to lift us above these limits. Yet never does our life's journey come to a final standstill. No amount of knowledge or depth of understanding puts an end to the questions of our mind. No object chosen or person loved provides a final stopping place for the longing of our will. The outreach of our thought and desire is limitless, extending beyond any finite reality.[9] What, if anything, is the infinity toward which we reach? Whence does our orientation arise? How may we interpret this thrust and the infinity it touches?

The fragility, loneliness, contingency and death

7

which pervade human life do raise the specter of life's possible futility and absurdity, suggesting that this infinity may be a dark nothingness. But there is also enough truth, goodness, integrity cour- age, love, and joy to summon a basic trust in life's meaning. These experiences suggest that this infinity may be the ultimate reality. We do yearn for a final meaningfulness to life as a whole, a meaningfulness that pieces together, harmonizes, and transcends all the individual fragments of meaning and absurdity. If this longing is not in vain, then the mysterious in- finity is indeed real, and is the ultimate reality be- yond all finite objects of thought and decision. The mystery out of which our hope for meaning arises and toward which it reaches is what is meant by "God." The word "God" designates the source and goal, the ground and terminus, which enables and evokes such a trusting response.[10] A person's actual, if implic- it, response to this mystery consists precisely in a trusting acceptance of and fidelity to this tran- scendent orientation. This response may remain im- plicit, a lived response that is not formulated in concepts or words. In Rahner's words, it entails "an accepting, hoping openness to the total meaning of hu- man existence";[11] a "radical self-commitment to the absolute uncontrollable in the act of knowledge and love."[12]

This orientation to the infinite, or limitless transcendence, is the deepest structural element, the most basic existential of the human being. It belongs to the very "heart" of man, a term which denotes, for Rahner, the one inmost dynamic core or center of the person.[13] It is a fundamental principle of Rahner's thought that the unity of a being precedes and grounds its multiplicity or plurality. Hence the heart is the one source and original unity of the whole person, prior to any differentiation into various capacities and activities. Yet the heart flows into these diverse aspects and holds them together in a plural or many-dimensional unity. The heart unfolds into intellect and will, into their corporeality and their activity in the world. It does so in quest of the infinite to which it is oriented. This transcendence is not self-initiated but already given with the dynamic core of the human person and situated at that core. One experiences this outreach, therefore, not only as drawn toward the infinite, but also as arising from and sustained by that very infinite. In other words, God may be grasped as that which is at once prior to our heart and beyond our transcendence.

We do not experience and know this transcendence from the heart or its infinite term as an object directly before us.[14] We immediately know and decide about the tangible world of things and persons accessible to the senses. The categories of our thought and language refer primarily to the realities of this world. At the same time, if we know these realities as finite and limited, we must somehow have glimpsed beyond their limits. We directly know the finite, but we do so in the light of an infiniteness which we discern as a kind of background. The infinite is like a background horizon or screen against which everything is perceived. Or it is like a light which illuminates everything else and enables it to be seen, but which is not itself directly seen.

The distinction between what is directly known and the horizon or context within which it is known applies to all our knowledge. There are also many

9

different horizons or contexts within which we receive our knowledge. Each intellectual discipline, for example, approaches its subject matter with its own distinct set of questions and its own distinct method. Our own underlying fears and desires also influence the way in which we look at events affecting our personal lives. Our horizons are the angles of vision or frames of reference according to which we interpret and evaluate the facts, situations, occurrences, personal and societal bonds which make up our lives. For Rahner, the final, absolute horizon is broader than and reveals the finiteness of all things. This horizon is therefore an infinite horizon. It is only when we perceive the finite objects of the world that we simultaneously discern the infinite horizon. Yet we perceive these objects as finite only because we discern the infinite horizon. Rahner describes our knowledge of the finite world, expressible in concepts and words, as objective, explicit, thematic, and categorical. In contrast, he terms our awareness of the infinite horizon as non-objective, implicit, unthematic, and transcendental.

Moreover, it is towards this infinite that our whole being tends. For if our experience of finiteness evokes a sense of dissatisfaction and incompleteness, then the fundamental thrust of our will and desire must be towards what is more than finite. No person or thing we directly encounter absorbs the breadth of our desire or fills the depth of our longing. No finite reality fully answers to our inmost quest and therefore none can compel our response. While our orientation to the infinite is not itself free, it is thus the basis of our freedom toward all that is finite.[15] This orientation also impels us

10

to seek the infinite in and through the world. Any finite choice will be made in view of the infinite and will contain a stance toward the infinite. A person will express his response to the infinite mystery that envelops his mind and will through his concrete commitments, decisions, and actions, and through the resultant direction of his life as a whole.

Furthermore, as noted earlier, this transcendence constitutes the very definition of man. As a result, the moral acts which either ratify or deny this transcendence will be invariably either an acceptance or rejection of who a human being really is, of the true self. There are thus only two real alternatives underlying and present to every free choice: acceptance or rejection of self and of the infinite goal of its outreach. Freedom is, essentially the capacity to opt totally and definitively for one of these two directions, and so to commit oneself completely and irrevocably. This idea of freedom contrasts with the superficial notion that to be free is to be able to make a series of successive, endlessly revisable, and arbitrary choices.[16]

A person may express a negative, rejecting option by trying to make something categorical and finite into an infinite: by deifying wealth, success, power, or pleasure. But this attempt involves a contradiction, and to pretend that what we grasp as finite is really infinite can only finally issue into despair. A person may indeed step into despair and judge that life is absurd, that man's pretension to infinity touches upon no reality, but borders an abyss of nothingness. The positive alternative lies in making use of things and responding to persons without making idols of them and thus closing oneself to the

11

infinite context in which they are seen and chosen. In this case there remains an openness to the infinite and a trusting hope that the silent infinity which surrounds us is the ultimate reality and the source and goal of unconditional meaning. Where such a positive response emerges to the level of explicit, full consciousness and expression, it becomes total commitment in adoring love, in which one falls silent before the immense mystery.[17]

Hence, the experience of God is the experience of that nameless and holy mystery in the light of which we know any finite person or thing and in view of which we make any particular choice. It is the oblique experience of that towards which our whole being tends from its very centre. God is the ultimate point of reference of this limitless outreach, yet God is distinct from this outreach and sustains it from the core of our being. The point of contact with the infinite will be this core and outreach. God is that which we touch upon in our innermost depths and our furthest aspirations.

Every concept of God which we form falls short and fails to capture this original experience of mystery, for our concepts are fashioned from and immediately apply only to what is accessible to the senses. The holy mystery is glimpsed only as the background illumination for, and goal beyond, the knowledge we have and decisions we make about particular finite persons, things, and situations. Nevertheless, the concrete content of our categorical experience will affect how we conceptualize this non-objective, transcendental experience.[18] Mystery will be articulated as the horizon and goal of this, rather than that, particular experience. To put it in more personalist, if anthropomorphic terms, the speech and summons of the infinite to the human mind and will, will be borne by the thought forms, language, and accent of the finite persons, cultures, and environments through which the infinite is mediated. The human response, both in action and in word, will also be conditioned by these same factors.

As we shall elaborate, Rahner comes to emphasize that the encounter with the infinite is especially mediated through the permanent universal structures of man and the world, and through the irreducible uniqueness of each person. God is thereby seen as the underlying ground of the intrinsic worth of the human being. God is similarly viewed as the final term of the summons to recognize and respond to that worth, both on the more intimate personal level and in wider social contexts. In Christian terms, the one who most truly, fully, and definitively expresses and embodies both call and response is the man Jesus Christ.

From what has been said, it follows that the categorical experiences from which the concept of God may be most adequately derived will be experiences which concern persons rather than things, and those which affect the deeper rather than the more surface levels of one's being. They will be the experiences in which persons are most radically and totally in touch with their own innermost depths and furthest aspirations. It is on the basis of such key experiences that the reality designated by the word "God" will take on a concrete, existential meaning. We may repeat, then, what was said at the outset: God is the mystery we encounter in our deepest human experience, in our inmost depths and in our furthest aspirations. This statement holds true in two senses: both insofar as

the transcendental experience of orientation to the
infinite is the deepest dimension of all experience
whatever; and insofar as the transcendent element e-
merges most clearly and can be most fully expressed in
terms of the deepest categorical experiences.

NOTES

[1]"Theology and Anthropology," <u>TI</u> 9, 28-45; "The Second Vatican Council's Challenge to Theology," <u>TI</u> 9, 3-27; "Die Theologische Dimension der Frage Nach dem Menschen," <u>Schriften</u> 12, 387-406; See also Anne Carr, "Theology and Experience in the Thought of Karl Rahner," <u>Journal of Religion</u>, 53 (1973), 359-376.

[2]On man's experience of himself today, see "Christianity and the 'New Man'," <u>TI</u> 5, 135-153; "The Man of Today and Religion," <u>TI</u> 6, 3-20; "The Experiment with Man," <u>TI</u> 9, 205-224; "Theological Considerations on Secularization and Atheism," <u>TI</u> 11, 166-184; "Experience of Self and Experience of God," <u>TI</u> 13, 122-132.

[3]"The Experience of God Today," <u>TI</u> 11, 164f; "Thoughts on the Possibility of Belief Today," <u>TI</u> 5, 3-11,20-22.

[4]"The Experience of God Today," <u>TI</u> 11, 160.

[5]"The Experience of God Today," <u>TI</u> 11, 152-160; "Theology and Anthropology," <u>TI</u> 9, 28f, 33f; <u>Foundations</u>, 14-23, 24-43, 51-71.

On Rahner's theology of mystery, see, in addition, "The Concept of Mystery in Catholic Theology," <u>TI</u> 4, 36-73; "Reflections on Methodology in Theology," <u>TI</u> 11, 101-114; "Mystery," <u>Theological Dictionary</u> (hereafter <u>TD</u>) (New York: Herder & Herder, 1965), 300f; "Mystery," <u>Encyclopedia of Theology, The Concise Sacramentum Mundi</u>, (hereafter <u>ET</u>) (New York: Seabury, 1975), 1000-1004; "Thomas Aquinas on the Incomprehensibility of God," <u>Journal of Religion</u>, 58/Supplement (1978), S107-125.

These considerations follow from and are rooted in Rahner's early foundational works: <u>Spirit in the World</u>, trans. Wm. Dych (New York: Herder & Herder, 1968) <u>Hearers of the Word</u>, trans M. Richards (New York: Herder & Herder, 1969). Both works have been subject to slight revision by Johannes B. Metz. For the changes made in the former book, see Andrew Tallon, "Spirit, Matter, Becoming: Karl Rahner's <u>Spirit in the World</u>," <u>The Modern Schoolman</u>, 48 (1971), 151-165. A translation of much of the first edition of <u>Hearers of the Word</u> is found in Gerald McCool, ed., <u>A Rahner Reader</u> (New York: Seabury, 1975), 1-65.

[6]Foundations, 32f; "Thoughts on the Possibility of Belief Today," TI 5, 3-9, On Prayer (New York: Paulist Press, 1968), 7-19.

[7]Do You Believe in God (New York: Paulist Press, 1969), 70. On the inadequacy of such a naive form of theism, see "Science as a 'Confession'?," TI 3, 385-400; "Observations on the Doctrine of God in Catholic Dogmatics," TI 9, 131-133, 137-144; Foundations, 61-65.

Two explicit statements of Rahner merit quotation here:

> That God really does not exist who operates and functions as an individual existent alongside of other existents. (Foundations, 63).

> If we are not to miss God right from the outset, the question of God must on no account be put as a question about an individual existent within the perspective of our transcendence and historical experience, but only as a question concerning the very ground sustaining the 'question' which we ourselves 'are', concerning the origin and future of this question. ("Observations on the Doctrine of God in Catholic Dogmatics," TI 9, 139).

[8]"Christianity and the 'New Man'," TI 5, 140-143.

[9]Christian at the Crossroads, trans. V. Green (New York: Seabury, 1975), 11-20; On Prayer, 31-44.

[10]"Thoughts on the Possibility of Belief Today," TI 5, 3-11, 20-22; "On the Theology of Hope," TI 10, 245-251; "Die Menschliche Sinnfrage vor dem Absoluten Geheimnis Gottes," Schriften 13, 111-128.

[11]"Marxist Utopia and the Christian Future of Man," TI 6, 65. In Christian at the Crossroads, Rahner speaks in similar terms of hope in an "ultimate meaning" that is "both definitive and blessed," and of an "ultimate and basic confidence in the total and all-embracing meaning of existence." (22).

[12]"On the Theology of Hope," TI 10, 251.

[13]On the concept of heart in Rahner's theology, as well as the notion of a plural unity, see "'Behold This Heart!'; Preliminaries to a Theology of Devotion to the Sacred Heart," _TI_ 3, 321-330; "The Theology of the Symbol," _TI_ 4, 221-252; "The Theological Meaning of Devotion to the Sacred Heart," _TI_ 8, 217-228; "Unity - Love - Mystery," _TI_ 8, 229-247.

The philosophical basis of this view is discussed in greater detail in _Spirit in the World_, 237-290.

The dynamic orientation of man from the core of his being is also explored in Rahner's writings on the topic of evolution: _Hominisation_, trans. W. T. O'Hara (Freiburg: Herder/Montreal: Palm, 1965); "Christology within an Evolutionary World View," _TI_ 5, 157-192; "The Unity of Spirit and Matter in the Christian Understanding of the Faith," _TI_ 6, 153-177; "The Secret of Life," _TI_ 6, 141-152; "Evolution," _ET_, 478-488.

[14]On what follows, see the references to Rahner's theology of mystery and also to his foundational works in note 5 above, as well as "Science as a 'Confession'?," _TI_ 3, 385-400. A short precis of Rahner's perspective may be found in Joseph Donceel, "Rahner's Argument for God," _America_, 123, 340-342; and Gerald McCool, "Rahner's Anthropology," _America_ 123, 342-344.

[15]In addition to the above references, see specifically on freedom "Theology of Freedom," _TI_ 6, 178-196; _Grace in Freedom_ (London: Burns & Oates/New York: Herder & Herder, 1969), 203-264.

[16]"Theology of Freedom," _TI_ 6, 183-187; _Foundations_, 35-39, 93-102.

[17]_Hearers of the Word_, 33f; "The Concept of Mystery in Catholic Theology," _TI_ 4, 52-54, 61; "The Experience of God Today," _TI_ 11, 162f.

[18] _Foundations_, 58-60; "The Experience of God Today," _TI_ 11, 157-159, 161f.

2. MYSTERY AS SELF BESTOWING: GRACE

Before turning to the God of forgiveness and healing, we shall briefly consider Rahner's unique theology of grace and the "supernatural existential."[1] Man's transcendence from the heart, he holds, contains within itself the hope of nearness to and union with the infinite mystery. "This dynamic force which the spiritual subject experiences within itself . . . includes within itself the powerful hope of achieving a state of ultimate proximity and immediacy to that goal."[2] There is an inner tendency to hope that ones deepest longing (however implicit) is not futile, but that a more immediate encounter with its infinite goal, in knowing and loving, is possible.

Since this hope reaches beyond the finite, it is necessarily a reaching for what is beyond one's capacity. It is a reaching to receive, an openness for a gift; it is a receptivity for a completion beyond one's grasp. In addition, this dynamism is always already present, and experienced as initiated and sustained by its goal. The tendency to trusting outreach, therefore, contains the assurance that the gift indeed has been offered. The very presence of the hope itself attests to the actuality of the gift. The experience of the infinite is thus the experience that what one reaches for is already given, in one's heart and in one's hope. A freely given gift, present at one's inmost core, connotes a bestowing love which is near. Hence, one does not merely experience the infinite as a distant horizon making possible our knowledge of the world, nor as a remote term far off beyond the finite persons and things with which our freedom deals. Rather, this nameless and holy mys-

tery, which grounds all truth and value, is an ineffable nearness and can be described in terms of
love.[3]

According to Rahner, this experience corresponds
exactly (in a mutually illuminating way) to the very
essence of Christianity. In fact, explicit Christianity enables us to differentiate the elements of
this experience more clearly. The central tenet of
Christianity is the self-bestowal of God as the nearness of forgiving love. This conviction lies behind
the doctrines of the Trinity and the Incarnation. The
absolute mystery (Father) bestows itself immediately
in a free act of love conferring forgiveness, healing,
and fulness of life. This self-bestowal extends into
the most interior domain of the human person, the core
(Spirit), and into the domain of human history (Incarnation). That which is absolutely transcendent to man
(Father) has freely become that which is most immanent
(Spirit). This presence within of total otherness is
manifest historically in the man Jesus, the incarnate
Logos. Within the heart of man is the loving nearness
of the totally other, transcendent mystery, which is
also embodied in Christ.[4]

This self-bestowal of God is the original and basic meaning of grace. It springs from what Rahner
calls the universal salvific will of God,[5] the freely given vocation to intimacy with God. This un-
merited grace affects the very transcendence of the
human being, the orientation to mystery, and thereby
leaves its imprint upon what is deepest in the person. The most profound truth about the actual human
being in the concrete, de facto graced order, is the
orientation to the nearness of the self-bestowing mystery. "The capacity for . . . the longing for . . .

19

the orientation to . . . the God of self-bestowing personal love is the central and abiding existential of man as he really is."[6] "In this self-bestowal, God, while remaining the absolute transcendent, nevertheless becomes the innermost principle, the innermost basis, and in the truest sense the goal of 'spiritual' creation."[7]

The deepest human experience, therefore, is graced transcendence, the orientation and vocation to intimacy with the triune God. In experiencing this transcendence (in and through categorical experience), a person likewise experiences its origin and goal, the gracious God as absolutely near. Only subsequently with the aid of explicit Christianity, does one come to differentiate the "natural" and "graced" elements within the global transcendental experience.[8] This transcendental experience is the heart of all religions, including Christianity. It is brought to an explicit stage of awareness and self-realization in the Judaeo-Christian tradition, which is regarded as the history of salvation in its narrower rather than more universal sense. In doctrinal and liturgical Christianity this transcendental experience is grasped as interior grace made definitively manifest and victorious in history with Christ.[9]

Yet Rahner insists that Christianity is precisely an articulation of the transcendental experience of mystery. Christianity is the articulation of the experience of a profound longing, sustained by a gratuitously bestowed hope. It is the experience of a gift which enables and a call which summons to a hope for a meaning and completion which exceed our grasp. The unfathomable and holy mystery which we touch upon in our hope, the mystery conferring and evoking that hope, is what is meant by the term "God."

21

¹On Rahner's theology of grace, see especially "Concerning the Relationship between Nature and Grace," TI 1, 297-317; "The Scholastic Concept of Uncreated Grace," TI 1, 319-346; "Reflections on the Experience of Grace," TI 3, 86-90; "Nature and Grace," TI 4, 165-188; "History of the World and Salvation History," TI 5, 97-114; "Observations on the Concept of Revelation," in K. Rahner and J. Ratzinger, Revelation and Tradition, (New York: Herder & Herder, 1966), 9-25; "The Existential," ET, 492f; "Grace," ET, 587-601; Foundations, 116-137. See also William C. Shepherd, Man's Condition: God and the World Process, (New York: Herder & Herder, 1969).

²"The Experience of God Today," TI 11, 153.

³"Thoughts on the Theology of Christmas," TI 3, 24-34; "The Concept of Mystery in Catholic Theology," TI 4, 54-56; "Immanent and Transcendent Consummation of the World," TI 10, 279-282; Foundations, 131f.

⁴In addition to the "Short Formula of Faith" articles cited in the Introduction, note 1, see also "The Concept of Mystery in Catholic Theology," TI 4, 64-73; "Reflections on Methodology in Theology," TI 11, 103-111; "The Essence of Christianity," ET, 196-199; Christian at the Crossroads, 31-36.

⁵"Universal Salvific Will," ET, 1499-1504.

⁶"Concerning the Relationship between Nature and Grace," TI 1, 312f.

⁷"Immanent and Transcendent Consummation of the World," TI 10, 283.

⁸"The Experience of God Today," TI 11, 154; "Observations on the Doctrine of God in Catholic Dogmatics," TI 9, 131f; Foundations, 129-133.

⁹"Reflections on Methodology in Theology," TI 11, 91-101; see also Foundations, 138-175.

3. GOD AS BETRAYED AND FORGIVING: INITIAL OVERVIEW

Within this perspective of the experience of God, we shall explore the fundamental experience of sin and guilt overcome by forgiveness and healing. In the light of the preceding discussion, we may already sketch a brief outline concept.

God is that which--or whom--sin ultimately rejects. God is experienced as the infinitely transcendent yet utterly immanent mystery which is betrayed by a negative free act of the human person. This rejection occurs through a denial of one's own inmost essence, one's true self. The negation itself takes place through the deliberate violation of a moral demand, a demand imposed primarily by the intrinsic worth of human persons, both individually and in social contexts. In brief, God is that transcendent presence at the core of our being which in sinning we ultimately reject through denying our own inmost self and violating other persons in the concrete deeds and tenor of our life.

Conversely, following upon the experience of this betrayal and its consequences, we may come to reach out for a forgiveness, healing and reconciliation. That toward which our aspiration ultimately reaches is what is meant by "God." God is the one who enables and summons to a hope for forgiveness in our heart, for a healing which repairs and makes whole our inner brokenness, and for a reconciliation which restores our damaged and distorted social bonds and relationships.

God is thus the mystery of love which at once offended by, yet forgiving of our sin, at once prior to and beyond our wrongness. God is thus to be understood within the very experience of guilt: firstly, as that whom sin betrays, and so as that before whom we are ultimately responsible; and secondly, as that toward whom we reach for a forgiveness at the core of our being and a healing in all dimensions of our being.

We proceed now to explore and develop the conceptualization of God afforded by this experience. After a few words to clarify the terms sin and guilt and situate them in a context, we shall focus upon the theological notion of guilt as fundamental option at the core of one's being, consider its embodiment in actions contrary to human dignity, and examine suffering as its intrinsic consequence. (Part B). We shall then turn to the process of forgiveness, first considering the possibility and nature of contrition and conversion from the heart, and next looking at its embodiment in actions which heal the person and extend the process of reconciliation to his interpersonal and social environment. (Part C). On this basis, we hope to deepen our understanding of the God disclosed in the crucial human experience of guilt and forgiveness.

PART B: THE GOD BETRAYED BY SIN

1. GUILT AS FUNDAMENTAL OPTION AGAINST GOD

Rahner often interchanges the terms sin and guilt, and does not always use them in a uniform way.[1] Guilt (Schuld) refers chiefly to a free act which goes counter to a moral value. It is viewed primarily as an act: an act which flows from conscious freedom and for which a person is therefore responsible, and an act which is expressive of a moral disvalue. In short, it is a free, responsible, culpable act. Sin (Sünde) denotes this same act insofar as it is a free decision which ultimately goes against the ground and term of man's transcendence, and is expressed in the violation of a moral demand. In traditional language, sin is an offence against (the will of) God. The notion of guilt emphasizes the freedom and responsibility of the act; the notion of sin brings out its affront to the infinite mystery. In its deepest theological sense, guilt is defined as:

> a free no to God which basically amounts to destroying the relationship of man to himself, to his fellow man, and to the things of the world . . . (which) strives in isolation to its own finality and irrevocability.[2]

Hence, the theological meaning of guilt coincides with that of sin. Both terms may likewise designate not only the initial free culpable act, but also the resultant state of enduring opposition or contradiction to God, self, others. Since Rahner himself exhibits a slight preference for the term guilt, we shall follow his usage.

The specifically theological concept of guilt at

once presupposes, differs from, and refines the everyday, legal, and psychological notions.[3] This is in
keeping with Rahner's view that theology, following
revelation, does not make statements about a realm totally outside human experience.[4] Rather, theology
clarifies and judges the concrete world in which man
lives out his existence. It provides a fuller context
and more profound meaning for the concepts by which he
interprets that existence.

In the socio-political sphere, guilt refers,
widely, to any breach of accepted customs, mores, laws
or conventions. More narrowly, it denotes an external
action contrary to the penal laws of a society. In
the case of a verdict of culpability, the civil judge-
ment or sentence assumes or attempts to establish that
the culprit was free and responsible for his actions.
Hence, both action contrary to civil order and free
responsibility are essential constituents in the legal
instance of guilt. A theological interpretation would
further insist that the civic transgression is a morally wrong action only if it does actually run counter
to the dignity of the human person, and does not merely disobey an unjust law.[5]

The requirement of freedom as a condition for
liability points, beyond objective wrongness, to a
more internal sphere of guilt. This sphere is susceptible in some degree to psychological analysis.
Besides the limits imposed by the very structures of
human nature, there is the pervasive conditioning exercised by further physiological, psychological and
sociological factors. These include genetic and he-
reditary factors, natural endowments, characteristics
of upbringing, social milieu, public opinion, coercive
social pressures, and the like.

These influences penetrate far into a person's psychic make-up. They limit and shape his or her freedom and provide the context for its exercise. Where they are negative, they can inflict such psychic pain and illness as to impel a person toward wrong actions with physically and socially disturbing and harmful effects. Inner conflict, suffering, and illness, which may lead to behavior destructive to self and others, comprise the psychological sense of guilt. Hence, morally wrong actions may be, in whole or in part, the unfree result of such influences, and therefore not culpable.[6]

Rahner maintains, however, that the realm explored by the social sciences does not penetrate to the innermost core of the person, the one root centre of awareness and freedom.[7] These disciplines deal with levels exterior to that core. Rahner sees these outward levels as accessible both to influences brought to bear from without and also to the imprint of free decision from the inner core itself. Inner conflict and suffering may indeed spring from undue external influences, from other persons, and from one's milieu. They may also be the consequence and expression of a free and responsible personal act, a result of guilt in the theological sense.

Certainly, the impact upon freedom of factors uncovered by the social sciences is perhaps much more far-reaching than previously imagined. If we observe, too, the seemingly senseless prodigality, ferocity and terrible catastrophes of the natural world, as well as the ignorance, cruelty, violence, slaughter, and horror of so much of human history, we may be utterly overwhelmed by the misery and apparent absurdity of existence. We may well be inclined to hold that the guilt of human beings, whether of wrongful action or of inner conflict, is something unfree. This guilt appears to be the expression of man as victim rather than as author of his own life.[8]

Yet, if the human psyche and behavior are totally determined, the human person is reduced to the level of a mere animal and any special dignity is negated. This dignity is inseparable from human freedom, from the orientation of that freedom to the infinite, and from its capacity for commitment, choice, and love. To protest against the "monstrousness" of nature and history as an affront to human worth is in fact to protest against factors which limit and negate human freedom and in that way deny human dignity. Unless we are to discount man as a distinctly human and personal being, we must allow for the possibility of a negative as well as a positive free act at the very core of the person. Such guilt would, of course, find expression in an inner state of suffering and/or wrong outward actions.[9] Since the core is oriented toward that which is called God, guilt in its deepest sense is a violation of this orientation and of the God towards which it tends. This is the theological sense of guilt.

Within this context, we shall now consider the theological sense of guilt, first in its core act, and then in its embodiment and consequences. The former is guilt in the transcendental sense, the latter its categorical expression. Since the transcendental is reflexively grasped through the categorical, we shall confine ourselves here to a basic perspective on guilt as a free act at the core of one's being. More concreteness and detail will emerge in examining the categorical expression of guilt.

As previously stated, freedom, for Rahner, concerns most basically man's fundamental disposition of himself as oriented to absolute mystery, not only as distant horizon but also as nearness of forgiving love. Yet this self-disposition occurs in and through moral choices regarding the persons and things of one's physical and cultural environment. Such freedom implies accountability for self, seeks an object of commitment, and has a gift character. These aspects help to clarify the meaning of guilt and the God it betrays.

If human beings are free, they are accountable for what they do. In situations where one's freedom is most deeply involved, one becomes more fully aware, if only implicitly, that this freedom and responsibility do not just concern this or that decision or action taken in isolation, but one's whole self. Such an occasion may occur, for example, when an individual understands a particular action as being unconditionally demanded of him, or sees a decision as having crucial importance and a lasting validity, or as determining the shape and direction of his entire life. In experiencing such accountability for his very self, the person experiences implicitly its ultimate reason or ground and that before which he is finally responsible. He experiences what is meant by "God."[10]

Insofar as freedom concerns one's very self, it can be regarded as the capacity for the total and irrevocable gift of oneself from the heart, that is, the capacity for love. In the final analysis, responsible freedom concerns the question of that to which or to whom one can and should so commit oneself. That ultimate value which is worth the staking of one's entire life, and which summons the total gift of self also indicates what is meant by "God."[11]

Freedom is also experienced as gift, as "borne and empowered by its absolute horizon,"[12] as rooted in the mysterious ground and goal of this free accountability and self-commitment. In experiencing freedom as gift, one also experiences the ultimate ground or source of this gift, and indeed of oneself as a free being endowed with an intrinsic worth. This, too, denotes "God."

Thus that from which we flow as free beings of innate dignity, that before which we are ultimately accountable for our whole selves, and that toward which we are drawn to reach and confide ourselves entirely, is what is designated by the term "God." This, once again, is the infinite, self-bestowing mystery which "speaks" through the concrete moral demand of a particular categorical situation. Our answer to this demand likewise expresses our response to the mystery.

As a negative act of freedom, guilt, at its deepest, transcendental level, is a refusal of that infinite, self-bestowing mystery from which we flow as precious gift, before which we stand accountable, and toward which our whole being tends and is summoned to freely respond. Such guilt is the spurning of a gift, the shirking of accountability, the dismissal of a call, the setting aside of a goal. It is a rejection of self in its graced transcendence and a rejection of the infinite mystery which is the source and goal of self. Guilt is "the total and definitive decision of man against God . . . which man can indeed experience in the depth of his conscience."[13] This act, too, will take shape in the contravention of a concrete moral demand.

As a refusal of the self-bestowing infinite on to which one's transcendence opens, guilt entails a stopping short of that infinite. It is a placing of oneself or of something else that is finite as the stopping point of one's freedom.[14] This is a setting up of "idols . . . on the altar of one's heart",[15] an attempt to make a finite reality into something infinite. At the same time, as we have already observed, this finite object remains something seen and chosen in terms of the infinite horizon. It will still be somehow grasped as finite and experienced as failing to fulfill one's yearning.

The guilty person thereby chooses a falsehood which leads to disappointment and despair, imprisons himself within the confining loneliness of the finite, and refuses that openness to the true infinite to which his whole being tends from its centre. In so doing, whatever the concrete expression, he experiences a violation of himself and has a concomitant sense of betraying something much vaster than himself. He has a sense, however obscure, of personal betrayal of an infinite presence, an infinite nearness. When Rahner uses more personal terminology (which he finds congenial with certain qualifications), he speaks of man's culpable desire to be God and to emancipate himself from the will of God who always wants man to be open to the infinite. The sinner thereby engages in a rejection of the free, personal love of God.[16]

Rahner insists that if the core act of guilt is to be free, it must somehow be conscious. There can be no unconscious, involuntary guilt. Only where someone sins knowingly against God can there be guilt in the theological sense. This, of course, in

31

Rahner's theological anthropology, can be an implicit, non-objective, transcendental awareness and decision. It need not take the form of an objective reflexive awareness of saying no to God conceived explicitly in categorical terms. We know but can never fully objectify what is in our heart. Our freedom as total self-disposition before God is transcendentally experienced. It is not an individually experienced datum alongside other objects, but is interior to and underlies all such experience.[17]

The transcendental act of freedom at the core of one's being does, however, express itself in the interior and outer actions of the person and in his physical surroundings and social milieu. This sphere is also susceptible to influences from outside the person. Hence, every expression of the original act of freedom remains not only an incomplete objectification but also an ambiguous one. As a result, a person can never know with absolute reflexive certainty his or her core act of freedom.[18] Moreover, besides being given little or no conceptualization, such guilt before God can also be forgotten, dissimulated, excused, or suppressed. Rahner regards self-deception and moral blindness as consequences of free guilt. He goes so far as to say that guilt can really be acknowledged only where there is an awareness of its being disarmed by forgiveness. Otherwise, the utter betrayal of self, others, and ultimately the infinite mystery would be too devastating to contemplate.[19]

When a person does find in himself the capacity to be honest with himself, to let fall his illusions, to admit his possible personal guilt, to fully assume responsibility for himself, and to do so without falling into despair, he experiences this response as something he has been enabled to make, as gift. That from which this gift comes to him is what is meant by "God". From this standpoint, God may be conceived as that which sounds, unveils, and judges what is in the heart of man. As we shall explain below, this disclosure is precisely in view of forgiveness.

In more guarded language, one may say that the recognition of theological guilt as a personal possibility or actuality implies the experience of a transcendent source which makes possible this recognition and simultaneously grounds the hope for forgiveness. God is that infinite presence within which man's guilt is encompassed, transcended and forgiven. The human experience that what is at the core of one's being is at once known, weighed, and, if guilty, forgiven, is the experience of God. However God comes to be conceptualized, God will be experienced as an infinite nearness which precedes and grounds one's freedom, evokes its total commitment, and yet transcends and forgives its most destructive use.

In order to clarify and expand these notions, we must now look more closely at the categorical embodiment of guilt, the fundamental option against God.

[1]For Rahner's use of the terms "sin" and "guilt," see especially "Guilt and Its Remission: The Borderland between Theology and Psychology," TI 2, 265-267; "Does Traditional Theology Represent Guilt as Innocuous as a Factor in Human Life?," TI 13, 136f; Spiritual Exercises, trans. Kenneth Baker (New York: Herder & Herder, 1965), 34-42; Meditations on the Sacraments (New York: Seabury, 1977), 42-48, "Guilt," TD, 198; "Sin," TD, 436f.

[2]Meditations on the Sacraments, 42. Note also the definition presented in "Guilt - Responsibility - Punishment," TI 6, 210, which may be cited here:

> Guilt regarded theologically is primarily in its most essential ground the total and definitive decision of man against God, the self-understanding of the subject in the 'no' against his supporting ground, and this vis-a-vis the horizon within which it is accomplished in 'yes' or 'no'; guilt in this sense is theological and metaphysical suicide, but one which does not thereby allow the subject to escape from itself into nothingness.

[3]"Guilt - Responsibility - Punishment," TI 6, 197f.

[4]"Revelation" is here understood both in the transcendental sense, as the graced horizon in the light and view of which man conceives of and decides about the persons and things of the world; and in the categorical sense, as the authentic articulation of this self-bestowing source and term in explicit doctrinal, liturgical, and institutional Christianity. On this twofold sense of revelation, see Revelation and Tradition, 9-25.

[5]"Guilt - Responsibility - Punishment," TI 6, 211-214; "The Dignity and Freedom of Man," TI 2, 235-263, esp. 255-258.

[6]"Guilt and Its Remission," TI 2, 265-267, 272-278; "Does Traditional Theology Represent Guilt as Innocuous as a Factor in Human Life?," TI 13, 137-139; Meditations on the Sacraments, 44-47; Foundations, 26-31.

[7]"Guilt and Its Remission," _TI_ 2, 277; _On Prayer_, 25-28; _Foundations_, 28-31.

[8]_Foundations_, 91f; _Meditations on the Sacraments_, 45. A particularly vivid portrayal of the negative elements which strew the course of nature and human history is found in "Unity - Love - Mystery," _TI_ 8, 236-240.

[9]_Meditations on the Sacraments_, 42f; "The Dignity and Freedom of Man," _TI_ 2, 254f; _Foundations_, 91f.

[10] "The Man of Today and Religion," _TI_ 6, 14f; "Guilt - Responsibility - Punishment," _TI_ 6, 201-204; "Atheism and Implicit Christianity", _TI_ 9,155-157. See also "Theology of Freedom," _TI_ 6, 178-190; _Foundations_, 35-39; 93-102.

[11]Ibid.

[12]"Theology of Freedom," _TI_ 6, 193.

[13]"Guilt - Responsibility - Punishment," _TI_ 6, 210. See also _Meditations on the Sacraments_, 42-44.

[14]_Hearers of the Word_, 33f; "Guilt and Its Remission," _TI_ 2, 269-271, 274f.

[15]"The Scandal of Death," _TI_ 7, 142.

[16]"Guilt and Its Remission," _TI_ 2, 270, 279.

[17]"Guilt and Its Remission," _TI_ 2, 267, 275-278; "Guilt - Responsibility - Punishment," _TI_ 6, 211-214; _Foundations_, 96f, 184f.

[18]Ibid.

[19]_Foundations_, 93; "Guilt - Responsibility - Punishment," _TI_ 6, 210f; "Guilt and Its Remission," _TI_ 2, 266f; _On Prayer_, 93-97.

2. THE EMBODIMENT OF GUILT

The core of the person, in its original spiritual-personal nucleus, unfolds itself in a plurality of powers and acts in the world in order to realize itself. Man is a being in the world who becomes conscious of himself and decides about himself only by becoming conscious of and deciding about an object other than himself. He comes to explicit self-possession in knowledge and love only by expressing himself in what is other than his core self.[1] "Only by passing out of the depths of his being into the world can man enter into the depths of the person where he stands before God."[2] Consequently, man's definitive self-disposition against God seeks to embody itself in a material and environment distinct, yet unseparated from, the real spiritual centre of the person.

The person himself, in the levels of his makeup exterior to the originating seminal centre, is the initial environment upon which this fundamental option is impressed. These levels include one's whole animated bodily reality, with its thoughts, attitudes, its whole psychic contents, as well as its physiological constitution. These objectifications of the core act spread outwardly into actions in the external world of persons and things, with its corporeality and history. (Everything in this realm is, for Rahner, connected with and united to the world as a whole, a world which he sees as a differentiated unity.) This self-expression in the "otherness" of one's outer dimensions and of one's world is the "symbol" or "constitutive sign" of the person's core and of its act. Hence, it is in this "intermediary reality" in which

the seminal person achieves himself that guilt is expressed and embodied.[3]

> The absolute definitive 'no' of the whole
> existence toward God takes place for reflex
> consciousness in perfectly determined con-
> crete acts of life. Sin takes place in sins.
> Sin does not take place in a merely transcen-
> dental interiority of the noumenal subject,
> but in the works of the flesh which are obvi-
> ous and tangible.[4]

The question now arises as to which concrete acts
of life are constitutive signs or symbols embodying a
self-destructive revolt against the infinite presence,
and as to how these acts might be determined.   In
treating this issue, we must keep in mind certain
qualifications to which we shall later return.   No embodiment can fully contain or absorb the core act of
freedom and each embodiment is also susceptible to unfree influences from without.   At the same time, once
posited, the constitutive sign does become somewhat
independent of the originating act and may exert its
influence even when that act is withdrawn.   Even if
one regrets injuring another, for example, the damage
inflicted may continue to handicap the victim.   Not-
withstanding these reservations, the connatural sign
of guilt is an action which violates the objective
moral demand of a particular categorical situation.
This violation may occur in two ways, insofar as each
of us is at once a human being sharing a common nature
with all others and an irreduceably unique person distinct from all others.   A concrete moral demand may a-
rise from a universal moral norm or from an individual
moral imperative.

For Rahner, the nature of a being comprises the
permanent essential structures which precede and make
possible the activity of that being.   For every na-

ture, such structures have their own laws, modes of development, and limits. The structures of the human being are especially those features which enable conscious, free activity. These do not exhaustively define a human being, who is more than a mere example of the species. The human structures belong in each case to a unique free center, who freely acts in and through and upon them, while remaining within their limits. Hence, Rahner distinguishes between the common elements and the unique center to which they belong. The former he calls "nature" and the latter "person."[5] "Man is nature insofar as he has certain essential structures of his being. . . . He is person insofar as he freely disposes of himself by his decision."[6]

One might say that nature denotes the raw material of man and person refers to the sculptor who freely works to shape and fashion that material. While nature is for the sake of the person, the free decision of the person must respect the laws of his own nature, just as the sculptor must respect his materials. The decision of man at the core of his being should be in accordance with the permanent structures, not violate or negate them. One form of morally wrong act, therefore, is an action which does violate these structures.

In Rahner's view, the features common to all human beings are transcendental elements which only gradually and incompletely emerge into reflexive consciousness. They do so as they find expression in a given historical culture and community. In an age in which genetic and social engineering are gaining prominence, the differentiation of the permanent from the historically contingent in man is far from obvious. Perhaps less belongs to the underlying human essence than previously thought.[7] Elements of this permanent human nature would include spirituality, intellectuality, freedom, unique individuality, communitarian and social being, masculinity and femininity, corporeality, historicity, orientation to the mystery called God, and in the de facto order of grace, orientation to direct personal intimacy and communion with this mystery, in Christ and the Spirit.[8]

The articulation of these structures constitutes a formulation of basic moral norms. Rahner sees such norms as comprising the natural moral law as modified by the supernatural existential, the graced orientation to the self-bestowing God.[9] Morality thus entails the discovery and acceptance of and response to the multidimensional nature of the human being, in self and in others, individually and in social groupings. The plurality of moral values is based upon the many-sided nature of man, whose facets only gradually emerge into explicit consciousness. These values can be spelled out in terms of concrete actions which respect or violate the structures of man.[10]

The imperative to act according to these objectified moral norms is, however, founded upon the intrinsic dignity of the human person. This dignity, while bound up with the nature of man as a spiritual and free being oriented to mystery, belongs to each unique person as such, who must not be regarded as a mere instance of the human species. The intrinsic worth of the human person is the root moral value and basis of all others. The fundamental moral experience, for Rahner, is precisely the experience of this human dignity as something absolute and unconditional, hence as capable of grounding an unconditional demand. It is because of this intrinsic worth that one must respect the structures of human nature. Each moral norm is an expression of the response due the underlying person. The different moral values to be put into actions are really expressions of what corresponds to that worth.[11]

While there are a great many norms respecting the dignity of the human person in his or her many dimensions, in the final analysis, these form a response to one being. The multiplicity of the human being, as we have seen, is neither a scattered, unconnected diversity, nor a mere juxtaposition of parts. It forms a plural unity in which all flows from and is held together in the heart or core. A response to any one facet of the person should respect that unity. It should be directed to the person as a whole, not isolated from or contradictory to that totality.[12] Yet it must not be watered down to a vague ineffectual attitude which neglects the concrete demands of particular persons, whether, for example, for food or fraternal correction. A morally good act vis-a-vis another person is, therefore, a specific action beneficial to one facet of the person's structure, in response to the unique sacredness of that person as a total human being. A morally wrong action, conversely, violates human dignity by its refusal to respond to a specific moral demand or by its response to one aspect of the person in defiance of the whole.

In addition, the specific action does proceed from and embody the one core act of the agent. As one being, the agent attempts to impress his or her fundamental option into every action and to integrate every action into that one central decision. The plurality of individual moral values and norms achieves completeness only to the extent that these values and

40

norms are incorporated into one's fundamental option from the heart and express that option. Again, this is a question of integrating many values, not negating or replacing them. As we shall later discuss, it represents a very gradual and never fully achieved task. In this sense, a person's whole life becomes an ever more complete realization of a fundamental yes or no to the infinite mystery.[13]

Hence, from the standpoint of its agent and recipient, its human origin and term, each concrete morally good action is, finally and fully, the gift of one's whole self from the heart to another human being in his or her uniqueness and totality. Now this is what is meant by love, regarded by Rahner as the basic good moral act, which underlies and sums up every particular moral demand. Similarly, the guilty action involves a failure of love, taking the concrete shape of indifference, neglect, refusal, and in its strongest form, hatred of another person or persons in their total humanity and radical uniqueness.[14]

To relate the above more specifically to the experience of God, we may first note that, for Rahner, unconditional worth can only have the character of gift when it is found in something finite. As finite beings, we cannot procure for ourselves or others an unconditional worth. We can only discover, acknowledge, and live according to a worth that precedes and is deeper than our recognition and response. Thus, in experiencing a concrete moral demand as such, we experience not only the intrinsic worth of the person which founds this demand, but also the source and ground of that worth, the reason why there is such an absolute worth. This is an experience of what is meant by "God".[15] Conversely, the experience of re-

jection of self or another in a concrete action includes the implicit experience of violating human sacredness, as well as the ground upon which it rests.
This too is an experience of God.

This dignity goes with being a human person; it
is rooted in and belongs to the very nature and per-
sonhood of each human being. The gift character of
this sacredness thus implies and is inseparable from
the gift character of human existence itself. It has
already been noted in discussing freedom that the human person as such is a precious gift. One's reply to
this gift contains within itself the experience of the
giver and one's positive or negative response to that
source. The ultimate ground and goal of the being,
value, structures, multiplicity in unity, and dynamic
orientation of the human person is what is meant by
"God." Hence, the one concrete human action contains,
first, the posing of a specific deed but secondly, the
taking of a stance toward human structures, human dignity, and the self-bestowing infinite mystery. These
two aspects are inseparable.

We must not, however, interpret this perspective
in too individualistic a fashion. The response to another as a whole person must embrace all dimensions of
human existence, physiological, social, and historical. This response must take place not only within
interpersonal situations, but in social contexts as
well. It includes the struggle to fashion a society
in which the individual in his or her uniqueness,
plurality of dimensions and wholeness is respected,
and personal growth made possible and fostered.[16]
The "voice" of God, as it were, comes not only through
individual persons as such, but also through the demands of one's social situation. The abdication of

social responsibility is a fundamental expression of guilt.

The permanent structures of human nature, violation of which entails theological guilt, do belong in each case to the irreducibly unique person. Each unique self may as such be the recipient of a personal moral demand. One may experience a moral task which falls to one precisely as a unique person, and not solely as a human being. Such a demand also summons the gift from the heart of one's whole self. Yet it is addressed to one personally, and involves more than the mere application of universal norms. We shall explore this dimension briefly and suggest some of its implications for the conceptualization of God.

Rahner holds that such personal demands may not run counter to any genuine universal norms rooted in the structures of man and his world (structures not so easily determined as was once thought). He does see these norms, however, as inadequate to determine every concrete action of the individual. There are situations in which many possible actions would be consonant with general moral principles, as well as other situations in which these norms appear to be in insurmountable conflict. Besides such instances, there is more to the concrete moral decision than the application of such norms. Insofar as each person is unique, so too are his actions unique and not merely examples or cases of general norms. While certain possibilities may remain open when judged by general principles, the choice of one rather than another possible course of action may be of critical significance for a particular individual. At the same time, such a concrete choice may be seen, not as a mere arbitrary selection from legitimate options, but as the coming to

43

light of one's own ineffable moral individuality.[17]

The structures of the intrinsically valuable person are certainly to be respected. At the same time, they should be integrated into and express the free decision at the core of the person in his or her concrete response to other persons. They are to be coordinated into the growth and development of the specific person as "this" rather than "a" human being. In this light, there arises the possibility of a uniquely personal moral demand over and above universal norms.[18] This demand may be seen as a summons to develop as this specific person through the order of love which one constructs out of concrete decisions. The study of the process by which one discerns the unique demand of consistent personal development, Rahner calls "formal existential ethics", and he underlines its importance.

The experience of moral responsibility as a call to act in this way and no other, even though many possibilities would seem legitimate, is the experience of a demand addressed to me in my solitary uniqueness. It is the experience of the ground and term of my own inescapable responsibility. I experience myself as addressed and summoned personally at the core of my own irreducible uniqueness. This is, so to speak, the experience of being called by name. As noted earlier, the moral call is also a call to an action which is finally to be incorporated into and expressive of love. Hence, such a moral experience is one of being summoned by name to love in a unique manner. As such, it includes, however implicitly and obscurely, the experience of being known in the core of one's unique being. For one can only be called by name if one is known by name. This is also an experience of being

44

valued and loved, since this summons is one which enables and calls to respect and love.

In this context, God may be portrayed as that from which I (and all others) flow as known and loved in my very uniqueness as a precious gift, freely responsible for the final shaping of that gift. God is similarly that to which and before which I am summoned to reply through categorical, concrete actions which embody the response of my own unique life. The infinite ground and horizon of my knowing and loving is thus at least implicitly grasped as the ground and horizon by which I am known and loved in my radical uniqueness, and thereby enabled and summoned to intimacy with this infinite presence.

> At least in his actions, man is really also (not only) individuum ineffabilis, whom God has called by his name, a name which is and can only be unique, so that it really is worthwhile for this unique being as such to exist for all eternity.[19]

In this light as well, the experience of guilt will entail much more than violation of universal norms and of their ultimate ground and goal. Guilt will be more intimately experienced as the betrayal of an utterly personal responsibility, a contradiction of one's own truest self. It will be in some sense grasped as the betrayal of the source of one's own unique being, meaning, worth, and vocation; a refusal of friendship and love; a personal rejection of a more personally glimpsed infinity. It will be a denial of the voice which creatively utters and speaks to that unique word of meaning and love which each human being is.

In more traditional language, Rahner states that

45

sin is not solely an offence against a universal divine norm. "Sin . . . is also and just as much an offence against an utterly individual imperative of the individual will of God which is the basis of uniqueness." It is a "failure of personal-individual love of God"; a turning aside from the "immediate personal encounter with the personal God as he is in himself".[20] In terms of our previous mode of expression, guilt is a betrayal of an utterly personal responsibility and of its source, the self-bestowing infinite mystery.

We may here summarize our inquiry to this point. Guilt is the free, culpable, and of itself definitive "no" to and personal betrayal of the infinitely near yet transcendent self-bestowing source and goal, ground and term, of oneself and others as known and loved human beings and unique persons endowed with meaning and dignity. Guilt is embodied in the violation of a moral imperative expressing the demands of the fundamental grace-transformed orientation to mystery, the structures of one's common humanity, and one's personal vocation. It takes the concrete shape of refusing the response due to another person or persons at the interpersonal or social level. Guilt is the contradiction between a person's embodied self-disposal and the true reality of others, self, God. It is the "contradiction between that in him which is free" and that which "he is intended to be and . . . inalienably is."[21]

The experience of this contradiction is painful. Rahner sees suffering in this context as the intrinsic consequence and constitutive sign of guilt. He sees therein as well the essential meaning of the notion of

punishment for sin. We shall now examine the consequences of sin and guilt and their implications for
the concept of God.

[1]"Guilt and Its Remission," TI 2, 269-275; "The Theology of the Symbol," TI 4, 221-252; "Unity - Love - Mystery," TI 8, 230-235.

[2]"Guilt and Its Remission," TI 2, 273.

[3]See references under note 1 above.

[4]"Guilt - Responsibility - Punishment," TI 6, 211.

[5]"The Theological Concept of Concupiscence," TI 1, 360-369.

[6]"The Theological Concept of Concupiscence," TI 1, 362.

[7]"The Experiment with Man," TI 9, 205-224; "The Problem of Genetic Manipulation," TI 9, 225-252.

[8]"The Dignity and Freedom of Man," TI 2, 235-246.

[9]"Guilt and Its Remission," TI 2, 274f; "Natural Moral Law," TD, 305f. On the question of universal moral norms, see also "The 'Commandment' of Love in Relation to the Other Commandments," TI 5, 439-459; "The Dignity and Freedom of Man," TI 2, 235-263; and the references under note 17 below.

See as well the two articles by James Bresnahan, "Rahner's Christian Ethics," America, 123 (1970), 351-354 and "Rahner's Ethics: Critical Natural Law in Relation to Contemporary Ethical Methodology," Journal of Religion, 56 (1976), 36-60, as well as his essay in A World of Grace, 169-184.

[10]"The 'Commandment' of Love in Relation to the Other Commandments," TI 5, 439-444.

[11]"The 'Commandment' of Love in Relation to the Other Commandments," TI 5, 440 et passim; "The Dignity and Freedom of Man," TI 6, 245f; "Ethics," TD 151f; "Christian Humanism," TI 9, 188-191, 200f.

[12]"The 'Commandment' of Love in Relation to the Other Commandments," TI 5, 440-457.

[13]"The 'Commandment' of Love in Relation to the Other Commandments," _TI_ 5, 440-457.

[14]"Reflections on the Unity of the Love of Neighbor and the Love Of God," _TI_ 6, 231-249, esp. 239-246.

[15]"Christian Humanism," _TI_ 9, 188, 201; "Atheism and Implicit Christianity," _TI_ 9, 153f; "The Works of Mercy and Their Reward," _TI_ 7, 268-274.

[16]On this theme, see "Christian Humanism," _TI_ 9, 187-204; "Practical Theology and Social Work in the Church," _TI_ 10, 349-370; "The Peace of God and the Peace of the World," _TI_ 10, 371-388; "The Church's Commission to Bring Salvation and the Humanization of the World," _TI_ 14, 295-313; "On the Theology of Revolution," _TI_ 14, 314-330.

[17]"On the Question of a Formal Existential Ethics," _TI_ 2, 217-234. On the topic of the uniquely personal moral demand and choice, see also "Situation Ethics in an Ecumenical Perspective," _The Christian of the Future_ (New York: Herder & Herder, 1967), 39-48; "The Individual in the Church," and "The Appeal to Conscience," in _Nature and Grace_ (London: Sheed and Ward, 1976), 9-38, 39-63; "Existential Ethics, Personal Ethics," _ID_, 160f; _The Dynamic Element in the Church_ (New York: Herder & Herder, 1964). See, too, the references under note 9 above.

[18]"On the Question of a Formal Existential Ethics," _TI_ 2, 225, 230.

[19]"On the Question of a Formal Existential Ethics," _TI_ 2, 226f.

[20]"On the Question of a Formal Existential Ethics," _TI_ 2, 232.

[21]"A Brief Theological Study on Indulgence," _TI_ 10, 153.

3. SUFFERING AS INTRINSIC CONSEQUENCE OF GUILT

We have seen that man's fundamental option is exercised in the rest of his personal make-up and en-
deavors to imprint itself upon his material, personal
and social environment as well. In the case of a morally wrong action, discussed earlier, a person's core
decision seeks to objectify itself in a way which con-
tradicts the structures, orientation and personal vocation of self and others within their external
world. As such, the attempted embodiment distorts,
wounds, and damages the outer levels of the person and
his environment. It violates the a priori and, therefore, ineradicable elements and these resist and protest, as it were, against this distortion. This contradiction is experienced by the culpable agent and is
necessarily painful. "It is the painful protest of
the reality which God has fashioned against the false
decision of man."[1] Insofar as this embodiment is
the expression of the core act of freedom, it is the
constitutive sign of that act. Hence, the constitutive sign of guilt is suffering, understood theologically as the painful "clash between reality and
guilt."[2]

The painful contradiction is thus a connatural
intrinsic consequence of guilt. Only in this sense
can we speak of suffering as punishment for sin. It
is not to be regarded as an additional arbitrary pen-
alty imposed from without. In this vein, statements
about "heaven" and "hell" are images which express the
absolute seriousness of present human decision in its
two alternatives. Whether or not "hell" becomes an
enduring reality for anyone, it brings out the possibility of suffering as the intrinsic consequence of an

irrevocably chosen contradiction.

> The radical contradiction between the per-
> manent supernatural existential, the per-
> manent offer of God's self-communication in
> love, and the definitive, obdurate refusal
> opposed to it by the free act will be ex-
> perienced as the '_poena damni_'.[3]

In addition, once the originating act is impressed upon one's own make-up and surrounding world, its
embodiment becomes relatively independent. It may
continue in existence and make itself felt, even when
the original act ceases or is radically transformed
through conversion. Ingrained attitudes and dispositions within oneself as well as the effects of a physical, emotional or other injury to another person may
persist, even if the initial guilty act is withdrawn.
These enduring expressions of guilt may continue to
inflict suffering upon the culprit and others. In
this connatural sense, they may also be termed punishment for sin. They likewise provide the context or
situation out of which subsequent new acts of freedom
must operate.[4]

These reflections help to shed light upon the
concept of God as judge of sin and as forgiving heal-
er. At the same time, they serve as a corrective to
all-too-common naive, excessively anthropomorphic, and
even destructive images of God. Within the experience
of personal betrayal discussed earlier, for which he
is personally accountable in his heart, a person also
implicitly experiences himself as judged and summoned
to conversion. The ground and term of this judgment
and conversion is what is meant by the term "God."
The judgment and call to conversion are not extrinsic
but contained within the very experience of the guilty
contradiction and its attendant suffering.

The image of judgment and punishment which is derived from penalties imposed for offences against the civil order does not apply here. Such an image would tend to depict God as an external judge who intervenes vindictively from without to punish people who disobey his arbitrary commands.[5] This view readily sees God as merely one particular being and cause alongside others within the world.

God must rather be understood as the transcendent origin, ground, and goal of the world in its totality, yet at the same time as a silently and ineffably near presence. If one is to regard God so conceived as judge and punisher of sin, it is not as arbitrary intervener, but as ultimate ground of the structures and orientation of man and the world.[6] In setting himself against these realities and therefore against his own true self, a person experiences the painful contradiction. He experiences the pain of betraying his own inmost self which is ordered to the self-bestowing infinite mystery. Sin implies judgment precisely insofar as it is intrinsically self-destructive. That before whom the person stands unveiled, accountable, and assessed in this contradiction is what is meant by "God."

Moreover, the very suffering itself testifies to the continuing presence of one's orientation to the mystery, an orientation which is graced yet ineradicable. The suffering persists as a call or urging to heed and respond to this graced orientation and its infinite term. The very suffering or punishment is thus a summons to repentance and conversion, and has a medicinal character.[7] Hence, God may be conceived as that before whom men or women stand accused by the very painfulness of their betrayal, yet also that by whom they are summoned to conversion so that the painful contradiction might be dissolved and they might receive forgiveness and the healing of their ravaged nature.

At this point, some further clarifications must be made so as to avoid the possible impression that all personal suffering springs from one's own guilt. The clarifications may also serve to further enrich the conceptualization of God.

We previously observed that the transcendental act of freedom at one's core seeks to express or objectify itself in the rest of one's make-up and in one's environment. Yet the originating act never fully embodies itself, and the objectifications do become relatively independent of that act. At the same time, the outward layers of the person and the environment are equally accessible to other influences from without. As a result, the same objectification may spring from a variety of causes. A character trait or a pattern of behavior, for example, may stem unfreely from the impact of other persons' guilt, from the pressure of one's social milieu, or from the weight of past human history. The outward expression may also arise from an earlier free act of the person, now renounced, whose effects continue to impose themselves. Or it may indeed be a constitutive sign indicating one's present or continuing guilt.

The same action, then, may be free expression from within or unfree conditioning from without, constitutive sign or external imposition, something done or something undergone, action or passion. To cite one of Rahner's examples, the same pattern of associations and psychic mechanisms could be set up both by voluntary training and by brain washing. Since our reflexive knowledge takes place by means of such objectivations, there is always a certain ambiguity in our thematic knowledge of our inmost transcendental act of freedom. We cannot be reflexively certain whether it is an act of guilt or of grace.[8]

Nevertheless, to the extent any action does in fact violate one's true structures, orientation, and vocation, that action will imply suffering as an intrinsic consequence regardless of its free or unfree source. Indeed this very suffering, as we shall shortly see, poses a challenge to one's present free act, as does the ambiguity of all our thematic knowledge in this regard.

As a consequence of this situation man experiences himself as at once responsible for, yet not explicitly certain of what is in his heart. On the one hand, he discerns that his moral responsibility and possible guilt embrace not only his external actions but also his very core self. He senses himself as weighed, not by appearances or even by ambiguous objectifications, but by the very decision of his heart. On the other hand, he also experiences the ambiguity insofar as he cannot be thematically certain of the core act of his freedom.

In this context God may be grasped as that before whom one stands not only as finally accountable, but as unveiled and weighed in one's very heart. In more colorful language, one might speak of the God who sees and judges the heart of man. At the same time, the objective uncertainty about one's actual state may occasion trust or anxiety, hope or despair. In the former instance, one (at least implicitly) trustfully

confides oneself to that before which one stands accountable, as to an ultimately trustworthy and forgiving reality.[9] The term "God" here points to that
presence which at once grounds and demands total self-
responsibility, yet also enables, evokes, and justi-
fies total self-surrender despite the ambiguity and
uncertainty.

Further consideration of the situation which precedes the person's freedom and provides the context
for its exercise serves to accentuate this perspective. This situation, says Rahner, is one in which
the free history of others, including their guilt,
plays a role. Indeed, it is one which is invariably
afflicted by guilt and its attendant suffering.

Man glimpses within himself the supernatural existential and other structures of his own being and of
the world. These urge him to positive moral behavior,
prior to his actual personal decision. Their violation incurs suffering as its connatural consequence.
Yet man also experiences a counter thrust, a reverse
urging, both within the elements of his make-up external to the core and in the surrounding environment.
This drive, too, precedes and influences his free
decision.

A person finds that even where his basic decision, so far as he can ascertain, accords positively
with his nature and person, he is still unable to integrate fully and clearly into this decision all the
dimensions of his existence. He continually encounters forces within as well as outside himself which
resist his decision, affect him contrary to it, and so
cause him to suffer. This painful conflict, which
Rahner understands as concupiscence,[10] is felt by

man to be something wrong, something which should not be, and is even more painful for that reason. Yet man also experiences himself as powerless to overcome fully this conflict.

The true interpretation of this condition is found, says Rahner, in Christianity. The human situation is always at least partially determined by the objectifications of guilt. As something universal, this guilt must go back to the beginning of the human race.[11]

In explanation, Rahner states that man is inseparably and in a mutually conditioning way both a personal and communal being. The human race is also a unity in its origin, essence, interdependence and goal. Furthermore, the overall situation, which precedes the free human act as its condition and material and which provides the context in which it is exercised, is a sphere which is common to all persons. The decision of any one person impinges upon that of all the others. Man thus springs from and continues in historical dependence upon that form which humanity had at the origin of its own history. This biological and historical unity means that man's situation here and now is determined by the beginnings of man, not merely as a chronological moment, but also as a unique basis upon which all subsequent history rests.[12]

The present situation of man, as attested to by experience and revelation, is not solely determined by an orientation to mystery as nearness. It is also affected by a thrust toward personal guilt, a thrust which is universal and sensed as something that should not be. This negative modification of the human situation must, therefore, go back to the beginning of the human race. If man's situation is always at least partially determined by the objectifications of sin, then, argues Rahner, there must have been an original act of personal guilt which infected the sphere in which subsequent freedom is exercised.[13]

This is what is meant by original sin, or the sin of Adam, whether "Adam" is understood as an individual or as a term for the originating humanity, monogenist or polygenist.[14] "Original sin", therefore, and the "consupiscence" consequent upon it, form a concrete existential of every human being. This existential exists in dialectical tension with the supernatural existential, the orientation to grace in Christ. Whether one opts for guilt or grace, the opposite existential remains and is the occasion of suffering. The positive decision meets with the resistance called concupiscence. The negative decision encounters the resistance of the human structures which it violates but cannot annul.

> Antecedent to the decision . . . man's sit-
> uation in relation to salvation is dialec-
> tically determined: he is in original sin
> through Adam and redeemed as oriented to-
> wards Christ. In personal free decision,
> the dialectical situation of freedom is an-
> nulled in one or other direction. . . . By
> either decision the existential against
> which the decision has been made is not sim-
> ply suppressed, for man in this life always
> remains in the situation of concupiscence
> and death and in that of having been re-
> deemed.[15]

The human situation is thus one in which a person not only lacks a fully certain objective awareness of his or her own inner state, and so must choose to trust or to despair, but is also drawn in two opposing directions. He or she is always in a state of conflict and suffering, which can never be fully resolved during life on earth.

As the objectification of others' or one's own guilt, suffering is never merely neutral. Suffering cannot be regarded in purely physiological or psychological terms as a personally indifferent happening simply to be deplored. It must be seen as incorporated into the total living of the person experiencing it. Suffering provokes, challenges, demands, and implies a reaction. Suffering is always understood and responded to in this way or that, and it thereby becomes either the expression of one's own guilt or the material for justifying faith. This is so even in the case of suffering that is imposed rather than incurred. To the extent that one's reaction to suffering is free and from the heart, this reaction is a fundamental way in which one expresses one's core response to or rejection of the self's orientation to the absolutely near mystery. However implicit and anonymous, this response will be either ratification of the sin of Adam or a sharing in the passion of Christ.[16]

Once again, in a human situation that is to some extent afflicted by ambiguity, painfulness, and the inducement to guilt, we are faced with a fundamental option: ultimately either hope or despair. We may despair over the final absurdity of human existence in the face of such evil and suffering. Or we may affirm that there is a basis for meaning and hope despite the pain of life, and that the acceptance of unavoidable suffering somehow has an enduring worth and validity. In this case, the final ground which enables and summons to primordial trust in the meaningfulness of life is what is meant by "God." To believe in God is to assert that somehow, despite the tragic tale of nature

58

and history, the ultimate source and term of all reality may be ultimately described in terms of love.[17]

Suffering, then, is an intrinsic consequence of embodied guilt. It is theologically understood as the painful contradiction between the culpable free decision and the true reality of self, others, world, and their ground, the self-bestowing mystery. Suffering is also universal, permeating in some degree the overall situation in which human freedom operates. From this perspective, God may be conceived as that transcendent presence at the core of one's being, before whom that core stands unveiled and assessed, a presence which continually summons to conversion, and to a basic trust in life's meaning despite evil and suffering.

We have explored Rahner's understanding of guilt as a fundamental option at the core of one's being, an option which seeks embodiment in acts contrary to human dignity and thereby implies suffering. We have also examined the implications of this understanding for the conceptualization of God. We may now explore the reverse side of this dynamism: forgiveness and conversion at the core of self, the extension of that conversion into the rest of one's person and world in the process of healing, and the hope for a total integration overcoming all contradiction. In so doing, we shall again focus upon implications for the experience and concept of God.

[1]"A Brief Theological Study on Indulgence," <u>TI</u> 10, 153.

[2]"Guilt - Responsibility - Punishment," <u>TI</u> 6, 216. On the notion of suffering as punishment for sin, see "Guilt and Its Remission," <u>TI</u> 2, 272-278; "Guilt - Responsibility - Punishment," <u>TI</u> 6, 214-217; "A Brief Theological Study on Indulgence," 150-158; "Punishment of Sins," <u>ET</u>. 1586-1588.

[3]"Punishment of Sins," <u>ET</u> 1587. See also "Hell," <u>ET</u>, 602-604; <u>Foundations</u>, 102-104.

[4]"Guilt and Its Remission," <u>TI</u> 2, 273-275; "A Brief Theological Study on Indulgence," <u>TI</u> 10, 151-153; "Punishment of Sin," <u>ET</u>, 1586f.

[5]"Guilt - Responsibility - Punishment," <u>TI</u> 6, 214-217; "Remarks on the Theology of Indulgences," <u>TI</u> 2, 194.

[6]Ibid.; "Punishment of Sins," <u>ET</u>, 1587f.

[7]"Punishment of Sins," <u>ET</u>, 1588.

[8]"Punishment of Sins," <u>ET</u>, 1586f. "Guilt and Its Remission," <u>TI</u> 2, 275-278; "Guilt - Responsibility - Punishment," <u>TI</u> 6, 204-206; "Justified and Sinner at the Same Time," <u>TI</u> 6, 223-230; <u>Foundations</u>, 96f, 104f.

[9]"Guilt and Its Remission," <u>TI</u> 2, 276; "Justified and Sinner at the Same Time," <u>TI</u> 6, 224, 229f.

[10]On Rahner's understanding of concupiscence, see "The Theological Concept of Concupiscence," <u>TI</u> 1, 347-382; "Justified and Sinner at the Same Time," <u>TI</u> 6, 225-230; "The Theology of Power," <u>TI</u> 4, 393-395; "Theological Reflections on the Problem of Secularisation," <u>TI</u> 10, 342-348.

[11]On Rahner's interpretation of original sin, see <u>Foundations</u>, 104-115; "The Sin of Adam," <u>TI</u> 11, 247-262; "Original Sin," <u>ET</u>, 1148-1155; "Evolution and Original Sin," in J. B. Metz, ed., <u>The Evolving World and Theology</u>, <u>Concilium</u>, No. 26 (New York: Paulist Press, 1967), 61-73.

[12]"The Sin of Adam," _TI_ 11, 253f; "Evolution and Original Sin," _Concilium_ No. 26, 66-73; See also "One Mediator and Many Mediations," _TI_ 10, 169-184.

[13]"The Sin of Adam," _TI_ 11, 155-262; "Original Sin," _ET_ 1152-1155; "Evolution and Original Sin," _Concilium_ No. 26, 68-71; _Foundations_, 109-115.

[14]On the question of monogenism, see "Theological Reflections on Monogenism," _TI_ 1, 229-296; "Monogenism," _ET_, 974-977; "Evolution and Original Sin," _Concilium_ No. 26, 61-73.

[15]"Original Sin," _ET_ 1154.

[16]"Guilt and Its Remission," _TI_ 2, 277-281; "The Eucharist and Suffering," _TI_ 3, 161-170; "Suffering," _TD_, 449f.

[17]"Unity - Love - Mystery," _TI_ 8, 235-241; "Thoughts on the Possibility of Belief Today," _TI_ 5, 3-11.

PART C: THE FORGIVING AND HEALING GOD

1. FORGIVENESS AND CONVERSION OF HEART

For Rahner, the experience of suffering arising from one's embodied guilt is of itself a summons to conversion. The suffering testifies to the continuing orientation of man to the infinite mystery, and therefore to the continuing self-bestowal which man's rejection does not abolish. This mystery may thus be described not only in terms of love, but of love deeper than and encompassing of man's guilt: forgiving love. Despite the threat and even actuality of guilt, it is possible to entrust oneself to the absolute mystery. One may recognize the terribleness of guilt and still hope for forgiveness and healing. In more personal language, the love of God is greater than the hatred of man, and so finds expression in forgiveness.

To really appreciate the "miracle" of forgiveness,[1] as Rahner terms it, we must go beyond a naive, superficial view of guilt as something easily written off. We must recognize its horrendous depths, radical inescapability, and hopelessness. Rahner underlines the irremovability of guilt. He regards it as springing from the very nature of human freedom, from the dialogical character of guilt, and from the enduring consequences of one's past free commitments.[2] We shall briefly consider each of these in turn.

The free act of man proceeds from his inmost center and strives to include his whole self irrevocably. The guilty act is an attempt "to integrate the whole of life into a no to God . . . the most terrible thing a man can do."[3] The removal of guilt would demand a free repudiation and reversal of one's basic option. Yet, if the original act has sought to incorporate the whole self definitively, it is not easy to explain how such a total transformation is possible. Such a reversal can only occur to the extent that the attempted integration does not fully succeed. The painful resistance of the structures of one's being and world, including the supernatural existential, prevent a total negative integration. While one may persist against these structures, they remain as a refusal of man's decision, a summons to become aware of and turn away from that decision, a call to repentance and change of heart.[4]

Nevertheless, it remains true that the freely culpable core decision has striven for finality. Hence (allowing for the reflexive uncertainty in such matters), the impetus to change of heart, and the actual change where it occurs, will be experienced as something which happens. They will be felt as gift, as surprise, as something miraculous. That from which this inconceivable gift flows is what is meant by "God." God is that which we touch upon in the experience of being enabled and summoned to recognize and turn from our guilt, and to open ourselves to the gift of forgiveness and a new heart.

The responsive act of distancing oneself from the earlier sinful attitude and action is the element in the conversion process which Rahner calls contrition.[5] This is not to be understood as an emotional reaction based on psychological or social factors, such as depression from loss of prestige. Rather, contrition is a free rejection of the moral worthlessness of the past action and attitude. It is not a

64

fleeing or repressing of the past, but a facing, ac-
knowledging, and assuming of responsibility for that
past.[6]

This repudiation may assume a variety of concrete
forms. It may be immediately motivated or occasioned
by the prior violation of any one of the multiple moral values which express the many facets of man and
which are rooted in his intrinsic worth. This multiplicity constitutes a unity grounded in the one source
of all values, the absolute holiness called God. In
repudiating any concrete immoral act, a person implicitly renounces the prior betrayal of God.[7]

As a distancing from an earlier decision, contrition implies or is itself contained within a new fundamental option. This new option is the positive aspect of conversion. It is the transcendentally conscious and free, religiously and morally good, fundamental decision toward the infinite mystery. This decision, too, may remain anonymous and implicit.[8]
Rahner gives a striking summary of such conversion as
an expression of a person's experience of and response
to God.

> Where a man is detached from self, loves his
> neighbor unselfishly, trustingly accepts his
> existence in its incomprehensibility and
> ultimate unchangeableness as uncomprehensib-
> ly meaningful, without claiming to determine
> this ultimate meaning himself or to have it
> under his control; where he succeeds in re-
> nouncing the idols of his mortal fear and
> hunger for life, there the Kingdom of God,
> God himself (as the ultimate ground of such
> acts) is accepted and known, even if this
> occurs quite unreflectingly.[9]

We spoke earlier of medicinal punishment which e-
vokes a response of contrition and conversion to the
mystery whose voice echoes, so to speak, through the

violated structures of reality. This view suggests a more basic reason for the irremovability of guilt: its dialogical character. Of itself, a change of heart does not bring about a cancellation of guilt. It must meet with forgiveness from that whom the guilty act has betrayed.[10] Of course, as already intimated, where a true change of fundamental option does take place, the gift of forgiveness and of conversion are already latently present as enabling ground. It is a question here of attempting to unravel the various strands of one global experience.

Every human act of freedom is essentially a response to a call, a call implanted in one's graced orientation to mystery, a call addressed to one by name. This summoning, mediated by a moral demand of one's categorical situation, and especially one's "neighbor", ultimately comes from the self-communicating mystery. Where there is a guilty rejection of that call, the resulting situation cannot be altered unless either a new call is uttered or the original call persists and remains in effect, inviting to a new dialogue.[11]

Where a person does recognize his betrayal, distances himself from it, and alters his nuclear decision, he experiences the gift character of this conversion. But he also senses that his turning back must meet with a forgiveness, which he cannot presume upon, compel, or give to himself. He experiences the need and longing for a forgiveness which can only come from beyond himself, as a gift from the mystery whose summons he has spurned. He reaches out to receive what can only be called a love which is deeper than and encompasses the wrongness which he himself cannot override. That "nearness of forgiving love"[12] toward which he reaches with the hope of forgiveness is what is meant by the term "God." The experience of God is the experience that one is somehow accepted, valued, loved and forgiven at the core of one's being, all the while continuing to be responsible and summoned to total commitment.

It remains to consider the third element of the irremovability of guilt: the continuance of the freely chosen past act into the present and future. This is the factor which can perhaps most easily provoke a person to despair. A man or woman can esteem that the dawning awareness of guilt comes too late, that even forgiveness does not alter what went before. He or she may fear being crushed by the overwhelming burden of the past. The longing for forgiveness entails what at first sight seems an impossibility: a longing for the transformation of the negative past, rather than its total loss or its continuing poisoning of the present.[13]

When a person posits a fundamental option, he seeks to embody that direction definitively in all levels of his being and in his physical and social environment. These embodiments become relatively independent. Hence, even in conversion, he cannot leave the past behind as something no longer real, simply cancelled out by a will to the contrary. Without being wholly determined, the present act does emerge out of the past, both one's own personal past and the past roots of the physical and historical situation. One's present act is at once a gathering up of one's past and a reaching into the future in view of the final completion of one's person.[14] This act contains one's whole past "preserved in concentrated form as the gathered experience of his life."[15] The know-

67

ledge gained through effort or suffering, the existential depth, the intensity, the freely acquired personal characteristics, the revolutions of one's life, the joys and sorrows--all of these enter as intrinsic elements into the present action and give that action its direction, depth and resonance. Even when someone freely undertakes conversion, or change of heart, he does so out of what he permanently is as a result of what he has been in the past.

This is precisely the problem where guilt has put its stamp on the existential realization of man. Even the present repudiation of past guilt still faces the continuance of that past into the present, as well as the repercussions and results of that act which cannot now be undone. A vividly real awareness of this predicament can provoke a profound sense of hopelessness. Even forgiveness seems a mere writing off of what can no longer be undone. This awareness is heightened even more if we recall that the context for personal decision is always and unavoidably co-determined by guilt, by the senseless brutality of human history as well as by the mindless cruelty of nature.

In the face of this experience, there is a very real possibility of despair. There always remains, says Rahner, "the terrible temptation" to believe that "something primitively evil, something dark and abysmal, belongs to the very heart of the essence . . . in us, or even in God." One is apt to regard and affirm light and darkness, guilt and grace, "as polar and mutually conditioning opposites, and to consider as naive anyone who does not think so."[16]

Despite this condition, and even implicit in its very painfulness for us, there is a profound yearning

of the human heart for a seemingly impossible forgiveness which not only disregards but truly redeems the
past. A person asks existentially whether it is possible to go beyond a sad recognition that the greatest
part of the potential fruits of his or her life is
lost. A person wonders if there is a forgiveness of
sin which "effects what we really are or could have
been or become without sin."[17] If one trusts this
longing for a forgiveness which redeems the past, one
experiences and believes in God, whether or not one
gives a name to this source and summons to hope for
an ultimate forgiveness.

> God would, therefore, have to be postulated
> as he who can in some sense remove an ir-
> removable and inescapable guilt of this kind
> despite its irremovability. . . . In recog-
> nizing the phenomenon of guilt and in hoping
> that it can in spite of all be removed, we
> must not simply take God for granted, but
> reach out to 'him' rather as the factor
> which makes it possible to have such a hope
> at all.[18]

God, then, is that which we touch upon in the experience of hope for a forgiveness that somehow redeems and heals the past. There remains, nonetheless,
the ambiguity of the reflexive awareness of guilt or
grace, the continuing threat of guilt posed by concupiscence and a sin-afflicted world, as well as the general continuance of the past into the present. As a
result, our awareness of and trust in the source of
redeeming forgiveness is always a rising out of sin
and into grace. In this sense, even the justified man
remains ever "simul justus et peccator".[19] His is
always a condition of reaching out of a certain inner
poverty and vulnerability for a grace and mercy that
transcends his understanding and control. "Over and
over again this life (of grace) rises out of the dark

depths of one's own powerlessness and into the ultimate light of merciful grace."[20] Contrition and
conversion are never once-and-for-all matters, but an
ongoing process. That upon which they are based and
toward which they reach is what is meant by "God".

Rahner does spell out his own theological interpretation of how the past can be redeemed, and we may
briefly note it here.[21] One's past, which does remain, can be taken out of its obstructing negation and
transformed and incorporated into a better and more
comprehensive framework. This is not a way of justifying sin as a necessary stage in human maturation, or
as an essential part of evolution, or as pertaining to
the hidden meaning of creation. Rahner unmistakably
views sin as "something radically evil and meaning-
less, something merely terrifying, petrifying and
killing."[22] Sin can exist only because it is contained in something more and better than sin, for otherwise sin would be sheer nothingness.

The guilty act does attempt to actualize one's
possibilities and integrate one's whole self and life
into a negative and false decision. In the process
one does actualize these possibilities and realize
oneself in some degree, even if in a negative direction. The more the guilty act involves the depth and
breadth of the self, the more complete is that self-
realization. A gathering, integration, and gift of
self is achieved which could and should have become a
reality without guilt. Yet the achievement does remain and can be incorporated into a right decision.
In this way, one's past is not obliterated, but transformed and elevated into the new fundamental option.

The past can be redeemed by including the integration achieved in guilt within a new positive option which ratifies one's orientation to the self-bestowing infinite mystery. Once again, that which enables and grounds this hope for redemptive forgiveness and which summons to repentance, conversion, and creative integration of self--that forgiving, transforming, elevating and healing presence is what is meant by "God." Contrition and conversion, then, constitute a new decision of the heart in response to a forgiving love which is able to redeem and incorporate the past.

We turn now to the process of healing, which is the extension of that core decision to the rest of one's being and world. This matter parallels the process of integration of one's fundamental option discussed with regard to the embodiment of guilt. Our treatment shall thus be a summary one, and highlight a few matters not previously stressed.

[1]*Meditations on the Sacraments*, 52.

[2]On this "irremovability" of guilt, see "Guilt and Its Remission," *TI* 2, 278f; "Does Traditional Theology Represent Guilt as Innocuous as a Factor in Human Life?," *TI* 13, 145-151; *Meditations on the Sacraments*, 48-52.

[3]"The Comfort of Time," *TI* 3, 154.

[4]"Guilt and Its Remission," *TI* 2, 278f; "Original Sin," *ET* 1154; "A Brief Theological Study on Indulgence," *TI* 10, 151-155; "Theology of Freedom," *TI* 6, 183-186.

[5]On contrition and conversion, see especially "Contrition," *ET*, 288-291; "Conversion," *ET*, 288-291; "Virtue of Penance," *ET*, 1187-1189; and also "Reflections on the Problem of the Gradual Ascent to Christian Perfection," *TI* 3, 3-23; "A Brief Theological Study on Indulgence," *TI* 10, 151-158; *On Prayer*, 83-97.

[6]"Contrition," *ET* 289.

[7]"Contrition," *ET* 289f.

[8]"Conversion," *ET* 291f.

[9]"Conversion," *ET* 292.

[10]"Guilt and Its Remission," *TI* 2, 279; *Meditations on the Sacraments*, 49f.

[11]Ibid; "Theology of Freedom," *TI* 6, 186-190.

[12]"Thoughts on the Possibility of Belief Today," *TI* 5, 20.

[13]"Contrition," *ET* 288f; "The Immaculate Conception in our Spiritual Life," *TI* 3, 134-140.

[14]"The Comfort of Time," *TI* 3, 145-148; "Experience of Self and Experience of God," *TI* 13, 129-132; *On Prayer*, 71-79.

[15]*On Prayer*, 71.

[16]"The Immaculate Conception in our Spiritual Life," _TI_ 3, 138f.

[17]"The Immaculate Conception in our Spiritual Life," _TI_ 3, 135f.

[18]"Does Traditional Theology Represent Guilt as Innocuous as as Factor in Human Life?," _TI_ 13, 146.

[19]"Justified and Sinner at the Same Time," _TI_ 6, 218-230.

[20]"The Meaning of Frequent Confession of Devotion," _TI_ 3, 178.

[21]This view is expressed chiefly in "The Immaculate Conception in our Spiritual Life," _TI_ 3, 134-140, and "The Comfort of Time," _TI_ 3, 147-157.

[22]"The Immaculate Conception in our Spiritual Life," _TI_ 3, 134.

2. THE PROCESS OF HEALING

Both the forgiving grace of the mystery and the responding conversion of man occur at the centre or spiritual nucleus of the person, at the deepest roots of his being. The challenge and task of an authentic conversion is to progressively extend that core decision to every sphere and layer of one's existence. One must integrate more and more all that one has and all that one is into a total yes to that freely forgiving presence which we call God. Indeed, the radical decision of conversion involves by its very nature the will to achieve this integration. According to Rahner, the gift of conversion is intended to draw into its sphere of influence the whole nature of man including its physical side, in order that all might be healed and sanctified. Conversion should also leave its impact upon the whole physical and social environment.[1]

The fundamental unifying force in this process by which man is matured is love. As we have seen, guilt is a failure and refusal to love. It is a rejection in some fashion of the intrinsic worth of one's neighbor which implicitly contains a betrayal of the self-giving mystery. The reversal of this process can only be achieved through love. This love, however, "is not to be understood as a 'mere sentiment', an attitude of mind, but as a power which gradually permeates the whole reality of man in his concupiscent and hitherto sinful nature, and orients him to God."[2] The very process of integration constitutes the mode in which love grows and develops in the direction of fulness.

The process of integration is usually slow and

painful and never complete during one's lifetime. In seeking to embody itself in the more outer levels of one's person and in one's environment, the original, central act of freedom meets with painful resistance. It meets with concupiscence and original sin, as well as with the lingering after-effects of previous negative courses of behavior: egotism, hardness of heart, pharisaism, cowardice, and other ingrained dispositions. These remain despite conversion or the level of integration attained within guilt.[3]

From this point of view, God may be conceived as the infinite presence which enables and summons to this integrating task, to the purifyingly painful struggle toward a love which accepts, gathers, and gives itself fully and definitively, and which does so without falling into despair at the incompleteness and painfulness of the task.

This precisely is a fundamental facet of asceticism, "the long period of ascetical striving" to overcome "all the secret roots and impulses of his sin" which remain even though repented. These include not only "those which simply belong to his lot, the circumstances in which man finds himself placed from birth onwards, but also those which effectively owe their existence to his own fault."[4] We may simply point out here a few aspects of the task of integration, not previously mentioned, which Rahner notes in his ascetical and spiritual writings.[5]

As a gradual struggle, never complete during one's lifetime, this integration entails much more than associating a vague thought or pious wish with whatever a person may be doing. Such velleities are readily divorced from a person's real life and have little or no effect upon the actual motivation and performance of the concrete action. Nor should a person unduly dwell upon self, attempting to analyse and dissect his or her own motivations. Rather, says Rahner, "it is better to try to purify and refine one's motives by looking away from oneself to things, and by letting oneself be occupied by life, others, and their needs."[6] He greatly stresses the ascetical and purifing role of human life itself, both in its crucial moments, and in the humdrum of daily existence.

People should give themselves to the multiplicity of the demands, tasks, and challenges of their daily life in the world, in accordance with valid moral norms and their unique personal situation, even though they cannot seem to harmonize fully this diversity, but must bear it in hope. They must attempt to respond to and live this "secular life" with integrity, constancy and fidelity, and be guided and educated by the inner motivation contained within the tasks themselves. They may be borne up on occasion by zest, interest, enthusiasm, and a sense of the value of what they are doing. At other times, they will be tried in the crucible of aridity, boredom, weariness, and futility, through which their complexity of motives may be tested and refined.[7] Rahner sums up this task and relates it to the question of God in the following way.

> He who responds to the world with genuine love . . . (whose) life in the world is lived joyfully, eagerly, earnestly, and bravely . . . with unreserved honesty . . . even without any explicit reference to religion . . . encounters in it the Cross of Christ and the inconceivability of God. . . . If he practices the virtues of the world and suffers himself to be educated by it in joyfulness, courage, devotion to duty and

> love . . . such worldly virtues will one day
> open to him the innermost mystery which they
> contain, namely God himself.[8]

At the depths of any of the virtues of life, therefore, one finds God. God is present behind the moral responsibility inherent in the tasks of everyday life. A person will grasp this matter more clearly, affirms Rahner, if he or she engages in solitude, silence, serious reflection and prayer.[9] The blending of activity and withdrawal, of speech and silence, which we only mention here, does reflect the discovery of God both in one's own inwardness and in the historical dimension; the discovery of God, in Christian terms, as Spirit and as incarnate Word.

Besides the realm of the everyday, Rahner draws attention to the fundamental phases of life and its critical moments, which he sees as so many forms or situations of conversion. Puberty, marriage, entering a profession, the beginning of old age, a profound friendship, proximity to death, and the like, all provide special occasions for deepening one's conversion or positive fundamental option and integrating it more fully into one's life.[10] These are the key moments, spoken of earlier, in which the underlying transcendental experience of God presses more irresistibly into one's awareness. Both in the ordinary and in the special moments of life, we are enabled and summoned to grow in the integration and healing process, by acting from the core of our being with a greater intensity and existential depth, and by (or better through) responding fully and appropriately to the demands of each situation.

This response to the moral demands of life is not merely a patient and passive acceptance or endurance of the circumstances, events, and trials of one's existence. The asceticism of today, in the service of integrative love, includes active social responsibility, "an increasingly effective responsibility of the individual within a society as such."[11] One characteristic of contemporary man is the capacity to exercise a greater mastery over his natural environment and even over himself, through the remarkable developments in the natural and social sciences. He has the opportunity, the task and the responsibility of more fully shaping his own earthly future.[12] According to his or her situation and condition, each person should participate in the attempt to build a better and freer world that is more worthy of mankind, more expressive of and responsive to personal dignity, more conducive to peace, justice, and love, and more restrictive of arbitrary power and exploitation.[13] This is a fundamental way in which people today are called to embody their response to mystery and extend its healing power into their environment.

This exercise of social responsibility is, once again, an expression of love of neighbor. Such love must be open to all dimensions of human existence, physical, personal, social, historical, within the unity of mankind and its history. It must thus assume, to the degree of individual possibility and opportunity, the task of building the human future on earth.[14] For Rahner, every guilty act in some way violates one's neighbor, if not directly, at least in the sense of infecting the common human sphere in which all persons act. Conversely, "every true conversion to God is only possible in the measure in which a man overcomes the guilt that he has committed against his neighbor."[15] The conversion and healing process must strive to reach from one's core to one's whole being and life and to one's community, extending in some fashion as far as the entire human community.

Indeed, from his studies on the history of the sacrament of penance, Rahner maintains that, in the explicit practice and understanding of the early Christian Church, it is specifically through their reconciliation with the Church that persons are freed from sin and reconciled with God.[16] The forgiving and healing presence which we call God is encountered and responded to in and through the graced community.

In a similar vein, Rahner interprets the so-called temporal punishment due to sin as the painful resistance to the attempted integration of conversion and its continuing incompleteness. The blotting out of this "punishment" by the Church must not be understood as the cancelling of a fine arbitrarily imposed from without nor the dispensing of a person from the process of a maturing integrative love. The Church's granting of indulgences must be interpreted, in this light, as the prayer of the Church that the individual may achieve this transformation more surely, effectively, and quickly.[17]

Through the asceticism of life, therefore, with its everyday duties, crucial moments, and specifically social tasks, the contrite and converted sinner exercises moral responsibility, realizes love of neighbor, and expresses a hope in the future. He or she thereby discovers and responds more fully, if implicitly, to the ultimate ground and term of such responsibility, love and hope. More pointedly, he or she experiences the basis upon which God is conceived as that which enables and summons to the healing and fulness of personal and communal life.

Yet, as we have already observed, conversion is a
continuous struggle, the integration of self is always
incomplete, the threat of guilt from forces within and
outside the person persists, and any society one
builds is always shadowed by finiteness and sin. Despite so many advances, "life today still continues
mysteriously to be the passion",[18] afflicted by
pain, suffering, anxiety, fear and death. We are thus
led to the explicitly Christian notion of asceticism
as the "sharing in the death of Christ on the
Cross."[19] A few considerations on this matter may
serve to round off our reflection upon the conversion
and healing process, and lead to the question of hope
for a total healing, wholeness, and overcoming of painful contradiction.

Both in death and in illness as the threat of
death, man is confronted by "passion". Passion is
here understood to be the necessity and inevitability
of death as something imposed from without, so to
speak, and confronting one's free decision from within.[20] In the face of death, the awareness of which
in some fashion permeates the whole of life, one is
forced to decide who one is and the meaning or lack of
meaning of one's life. Here again, the stark alternatives are hope and despair: despair at the ultimate
futility of a life that ends in death; hope for an enduring meaning and validity of life despite death.
The ground and goal of such hope for enduring validity
is what is meant by "God."[21]

Rahner points to certain trends in a consumer society which do tend to express and push one in the direction of futility and despair. Where one is exces-

sively weighed down by anxiety over death, one is prone to excesses such as immoderate greed and acquisitiveness, insatiable hedonism, and lust for power. These, too, prevent the capacity for renunciation and concern for others in a practical down-to-earth way which is essential to the exercise of social responsibility.[22] On the other hand, a hope for enduring meaning despite death does find expression in a genuine social concern. Such hope both recognizes the non-ultimacy of any social structures and so is free to let them pass. It is also necessarily embodied in a love of neighbor in all dimensions of existence including the social.[23]

Yet the reality and painfulness of death vividly bring home the fact that life is incomplete and that one is unable to abolish all sorrow. The mortality of self, others, every culture, and the physical universe itself makes clear their finiteness, as does the painful contradiction arising from guilt which one cannot fully overcome even when forgiven and converted. This finiteness, colored by guilt and death, is nonetheless a finiteness which is grasped in the light of the infinite towards which the human person tends.

We are thus brought back to the first section of this study. The essence of man is orientation to the infinite. It is openness to the self-bestowal of the infinite mystery. The deepest element in man is his graced orientation and vocation to intimacy with God. In the light of our subsequent considerations, we have been able to sketch further aspects of this human transcendence of man.

Man is liable to betray his vocation through guilt at the core of his being, is unable to integrate a positive decision or conversion fully into his whole being and world, is afflicted by the sins of humanity, and is subject to suffering and death. His outreach from the heart is thus a reaching, in part, out of wrongness, woundedness, and incompleteness, for a forgiveness, healing, wholeness, and fulness of life which can only come as a gift. (This, of course, is an outreach that must come from a self which strives to gather and give itself individually and socially; an outreach in and through and beyond the finite.) That which sustains this hope and that toward which it reaches is what is meant by "God." God is the ground and goal of a meaning and hope and love that is deeper and greater than guilt, death, and suffering, an infinite presence from which flows forgiveness, healing, and fulness of life.

This, too, is the essential teaching of Christianity. The infinite mystery, the Father, is absolutely near in the heart of man through the gift of his Spirit, and visibly manifest in the man Jesus, who died for our sins and rose that we might have the fulness of life. To maintain and live this hope is to believe in the Father, receive the Spirit, and participate in the death and resurrection of the Son. "The genuine Christian attitude prescribes that . . . we reach out of hope toward that future which is constituted by the compassion of God."[24]

[1]On the process of integration, see especially "A Brief Theological Study on Indulgence," _TI_ 10, 150-165; and, in addition, "Remarks on the Theology of Indulgence," _TI_ 196-199; "The Commandment of Love in Relation to the Other Commandments," _TI_ 5, 439-459; "On the Official Teaching of the Church Today on the Subject of Indulgences," _TI_ 10, 184-198.

[2]"On the Official Teaching of the Church Today on the Subject of Indulgences," _TI_ 10, 190.

[3]"A Brief Theological Study on Indulgence," _TI_ 10, 151-158.

[4]"A Brief Theological Study on Indulgence," _TI_ 10, 156.

[5]Major collections of Rahner's spiritual writings include _TI_ 3, 7, and 8; _Opportunities for Faith, Elements of a Modern Spirituality_, trans. E. Quinn (New York: Seabury, 1974); and _Spiritual Exercises_.

[6]"Some Thoughts on 'a Good Intention'," _TI_ 3, 128. See the entire article, 105-128.

[7]"Some Thoughts on 'a Good Intention'," _TI_ 3, 125-128.

[8]"Christian Living Formerly and Today," _TI_ 7, 17.

[9]"Christian Living Formerly and Today," _TI_ 7, 3-24; "Thoughts on the Theology of Christmas," _TI_ 3, 24-29, _Christian at the Crossroads_, 48-61.

[10]"Reflections on the Problem of the Gradual Ascent to Christian Perfection," _TI_ 3, 3-23, esp. 15-23; "Conversion," _ET_ 292-294.

[11]_Christian at the Crossroads_, 80. On the relation of penance, contrition, conversion, and asceticism, to social responsibility, see especially 75-83; "Christian Living Formerly and Today _TI_ 7, 16-24.

[12]On this mastery of nature, see "Christianity and the 'New Man'," _TI_ 5, 135-153; "The Man of Today and Religion," _TI_ 6, 3-20; "The Experiment with Man,"

<u>TI</u> 9, 205-224; "The Problem of Genetic Manipulation," <u>TI</u> 225-252.

¹³On the question of social responsibility it-self, see the references under Part B, 2, note 16.

¹⁴"Christian Humanism," <u>TI</u> 9, 188-190; "The Church's Commission to Bring Salvation and the Humani-zation of the World," <u>TI</u> 14, 308-313; "On the Theology of Revolution," <u>TI</u> 14, 316f.

¹⁵<u>Meditations on the Sacraments</u>, 55. See also 53-59; <u>Christian at the Crossroads</u>, 75-77; "On the Of-ficial Teaching of the Church Today on the Subject of Indulgences," <u>TI</u> 10, 186-190.

¹⁶"Penance as an Additional Act of Reconcilia-tion with Church," <u>TI</u> 10, 125-149; "Forgotten Truths Concerning the Sacrament of Penance," <u>TI</u> 2, 135-174; "Penance," <u>ET</u>, 1189-1204' and the entire <u>Schriften</u> 11.

¹⁷"A Brief Theological Study on Indulgence," <u>TI</u> 158-165; "Remarks on the Theology of Indulgence," <u>TI</u> 194-198; "On the Offical Teaching of the Church Today on the subject of Indulgences," <u>TI</u> 10, 186-198.

¹⁸"Christian Living Formerly and Today," <u>TI</u> 7, 21.

¹⁹"Christian Living Formerly and Today," <u>TI</u> 7, 21. On this dimension of asceticism, see "Reflections on the Theology of Renunciation," <u>TI</u> 3, 47-57; "The Passion and Asceticism," <u>TI</u> 3, 58-85; "Self-Realiza-tion and Taking Up One's Cross," <u>TI</u> 9, 253-257; "Nachfolge des Gekreuzigten," <u>Schriften</u> 13, 188-203.

²⁰"The Passion and Asceticism," <u>TI</u> 3, 69-73.

²¹"The Passion and Asceticism," <u>TI</u> 3, 74-82. On Rahner's treatment of death, see especially <u>On the Theology of Death</u>, trans. C. Henkey (Freiberg: Herder/Montreal: Palm, 1961); "Dogmatic Questions on Easter," <u>TI</u> 4, 127-133; "The Life of the Dead," <u>TI</u> 4, 347-354; "The Scandal of Death," <u>TI</u> 17, 140-144; "On Christian Dying," <u>TI</u> 7, 285-293; "Theological Consid-erations Concerning the Moment of Death," <u>TI</u> 11, 309-321; "Ideas for a Theology of Death," <u>TI</u> 13, 169-186; "Das Christliche Sterben," <u>Schriften</u> 13, 269-304; "Death," <u>ET</u>, 329-333.

On Rahner's treatment of illness as anticipation of death, and as affliction from without which provokes a free attitude from within; and on the healing process, which is to extend to all dimensions of one's being and world, see: "The Saving Force and Healing Power of Faith," _TI_ 5, 460-467; "Proving Oneself in Time of Sickness," _TI_ 7, 275-284; "Die Freiheit des Kranken in Theologischer Sicht," _Schriften_ 12, 439-454; _Meditations_ _on_ _the_ _Sacraments_, 79-93.

[22]"Christian Living Formerly and Today," _TI_ 7, 20-22. See also "The Theology of Poverty," _TI_ 8, 168-214; "The Unreadiness of the Church's Members to Accept Poverty," _TI_ 14, 270-279.

[23]"Christianity and the 'New Man'," _TI_ 5, 135-153; "On the Theology of Hope," _TI_ 10, 242-259; _Christian_ _at_ _the_ _Crossroads_, 87-93. See also the references under Part B, 2, note 16.

[24]"Does Traditional Theology Represent Guilt as Innocuous as a Factor in Human Life?," _TI_ 13, 139. On the essential core of Christianity, see references under Part A, 2, note 4.

CONCLUSION

Through the many writings of Karl Rahner, largely occasioned by his perception of crucial issues, we have pursued one of the central tenets of his theology: God is the infinite mystery bestowed as the nearness of forgiving love; and man is openness and orientation to this mystery. We have examined this dialectical polarity of divine bestowal and human response in one of the critical areas of experience: human guilt and suffering before divine forgiveness and healing. By way of conclusion, we shall add a few words of appraisal and comment.

Rahner is attempting to bring together human experience and Christian doctrine and to discern the connections between them. The fundamental link is found in his theology of mystery. The deepest human experience is man's orientation to the infinite. This experience of mystery receives its fullest interpretation and clearest articulation in explicit Christianity. At the same time, explicit Christianity must be seen as referring precisely to that experienced mystery. God is the mystery encountered in our deepest human experience. The God so encountered is the Father of Jesus Christ and Giver of the Spirit. Hence, doctrine and experience should be mutually illuminating and correcting.

Rahner approaches this theological task with the tools of what he terms his transcendental theological anthropology.[1] He seeks to explore the conditions of possibility of experience and revelation. He admits that this is one of many possible approaches in an age of pluralism in theology as well as in other spheres of life. Yet he stresses that one must follow some method, and must attempt to justify, clarify, and apply that method consistently in one's investigations. Rahner sees the transcendental approach as particularly fruitful. The challenge to a theologian who would differ is to offer another approach which would at once shed more light on the subject considered and prove more true to reality.

Behind Rahner's attempts to link Christianity and experience in the light of a transcendental method, lies a vision of great depth, comprehensiveness and consistency. This overarching vision is presupposed and brought to bear on any topic he is considering, and the particular topic in its turn serves to further illuminate that basic perspective.

Yet this vision is of an almost incredible simplicity. Rahner states in effect that the heart of man is a hunger for the infinite, and that this hunger is not in vain. We might put it in terms more specific to the topic we have been considering. It is possible to live in hope despite evil: such hope is a gift: its source is what is meant by "God."

Rahner looks to the human experience reflected in so much of religion, art, and literature. This is the experience of quest, of longing, of reaching out, a restlessness that takes us beyond all we encounter and choose towards something infinite. This quest is for a meaning that is ultimate. To this human outreach from the heart, the only alternatives are, finally, hope or despair. The source and goal of this hope is what is meant by "God." God is the ground out of which this hope arises and the horizon toward which it reaches. The question of God is not a casual intellectual inquiry about a possible existent. It is a life and death quest that arises out of the depths of one's being.

Rahner's interpretation also avoids the two extremes in which God is usually consigned to nonreality. One view divorces God totally from human experience. It is found in certain naive forms of theism and atheism, where God is portrayed as one object or item among many others whom a person may or may not come across in his or her journey through life. In the other extreme view, God is totally reduced to human experience, of which he is a projection. In Rahner's view, both immanence and transcendence are preserved. As the mystics have said, God is at the core of one's being. But what is at the core is totally other. The deepest human experiences are our points of contact, as it were, with God. But what these experiences touch upon is utterly transcendent, and evokes adoring silence.

Rahner's vision of a near yet transcendent source of meaning and hope is likewise far removed from a superficial or sentimental view which neglects the horrifying elements of existence. This fact should be clear from the whole preceding presentation. From his earliest writings, Rahner exhibits a very strong awareness of the elements of darkness, suffering and evil in human life. He faces these squarely without falling into despair, while recognizing this as a distinct possibility.

Rahner concentrates upon the experience and image of man as a being who reaches beyond himself from the core, and correspondingly presents God as ground and term of that transcendence. This focus allows for a nuanced interpretation of a variety of human experiences and of the concept of God they suggest. Because man's reaching beyond himself springs from an orientation that is already there in the core of his being, man experiences himself as at once gifted and called, as enabled and summoned, as endowed with a dignity and with a vocation. He is thereby able to conceptualize God both as source of gift and as goal of summons, as that from which and to which he reaches.

More specifically, man experiences himself as a gift of intrinsic value, yet given into his own hands as raw material for which he is accountable, and called by name to fashion that self into an enduring work of art by responding to others personally and socially. Yet at the same time man is inclined to refuse this task, to distort the material and to reject the others. In other words, man experiences himself to some extent as gifted, responsible, judged, guilty, forgiven and healed. This experience implies a source and term of the gift and call. This is what is meant by "God."

The above terms are all personal and so Rahner speaks of God in personal terms, as does much of the language of the Christian tradition. Yet to speak of God as self-bestowing, is in fact to articulate the experience of being gifted and addressed and, of course, the experience of a source and summons. Yet the point of contact remains the human experience. That from which the gift and call come is what is meant by "God." Perhaps one cannot nor need not say more.

Rahner faces this particular point, and asserts that God is experienced only as ground and not as direct object, only as horizon and not as that which is

seen within the horizon. He adds, too, that man experiences God as ground of himself precisely as conscious and free personal being. While one must not
attribute to God the limitations found in finite sub-
jectivity, nevertheless, that which grounds the person
cannot be less than personal. God cannot be portrayed
in models taken from the impersonal world of things as
a kind of unconscious and impersonal cosmic law.
Rahner makes the final observation that the more concrete meaning of the concept of God as person must be
determined through personal experience in the depths
of one's conscience, through the historical experience
of the human race, and in particular through the history of the Christian revelation.[2]

This may well be the case. Yet with the qualifications drawn to avoid a naive theism (or atheism),
with the recognition that one's experience does touch
a reality distinct from that experience, and in terms
of it, one may also demonstrate a great deal of re-
serve in speaking of God as _a_ person, in too anthropomorphic a fashion. One may also state, as at least
intimated in Rahner's view of the relationship between
doctrine and experience, that more is involved than
filling out the content of the infinitely near mystery
by the explicit Christian tradition. In a correspond-
ing manner, the statements of the Christian tradition
may themselves even be clarified and their interpretation refined precisely by the profound experience of
and disciplined reflection upon the dimension of the
infinite mystery.

In any event, Rahner raises the fundamental human
question: is hope possible in spite of evil? And he
provides a positive answer that is at once simple and

profound, comprehensive and unified, austere and at-
tractive, realistic and compassionate. One cannot ask
more of any theologian.

NOTES

[1]On Rahner's theological method, see especially "Theology and Anthropology," TI 9, 28-45; "Reflections on Methodology in Theology," TI 11, 68-114; "Pluralism in Theology and the Unity of the Creed in the Church," TI 11, 3-23; "Possible Courses for the Theology of the Future," TI 13, 32-60; "The Current Relationship between Philosophy and Theology," TI 13, 61-79; "Formal and Fundamental Theology," ET, 524f; "Philosophy and Theology," ET, 1228-1233; "Theology," ET, 1686-1701; "Transcendental Theology," ET, 1748-1751; Foundations, 3-25.

See also Anne Carr, The Theological Method of Karl Rahner (Missoula, MT: Scholar's Press, 1977); Louis Roberts, The Achievement of Karl Rahner (New York: Herder and Herder, 1966), esp, 7-51; and William Dych, "Theology in a New Key," A World of Grace, 1-16.

[2]Foundations, 71-75.